TWAYNE'S WORLD AUTHOR SERIES

A Survey of the World's Literature

Sylvia E. Bowman, Indiana University

GENERAL EDITOR

GUATEMALA

John P. Dyson, Indiana University

EDITOR

Miguel Angel Asturias

(TWAS 122)

TWAYNE'S WORLD AUTHORS SERIES (TWAS)

The purpose of TWAS is to survey the major writers —novelists, dramatists, historians, poets, philosophers, and critics—of the nations of the world. Among the national literatures covered are those of Australia, Canada, China, Eastern Europe, France, Germany, Greece, India, Italy, Japan, Latin America, New Zealand, Poland, Russia, Scandinavia, Spain, and the African nations, as well as Hebrew, Yiddish, and Latin Classical literatures. This survey is complemented by Twayne's United States Authors Series and English Authors Series.

The intent of each volume in these series is to present a critical-analytical study of the works of the writer; to include biographical and historical material that may be necessary for understanding, appreciation, and critical appraisal of the writer; and to present all material in clear, concise English—but not to vitiate the scholarly content of the work by doing so.

Miguel Angel Asturias

By RICHARD J. CALLAN

University of New Hampshire

Twayne Publishers, Inc.   ::   New York

MIGUEL ANGEL ASTURIAS

by

RICHARD CALLAN

This study of the Guatemalan novelist and Nobel Prize recipient Miguel Angel Asturias, analyzes his first five novels, his plays and a selection of his short stories.

The stated objective of Asturias in his fiction is to portray the reality of his country, be it social or political, and to retell its myths and legends, especially those that still mold the thinking of the people. The novels *El Señor Presidente* and *Hombres de maíz,* typical of these two veins respectively and the avowed favorites of their author, receive the most detailed attention here (over a third of the book) in order to illustrate the singular manner and techniques by which Asturias enriches the texture of his works and multiplies their levels of meaning; for in addition to the vibrant and complex world depicted in the surface plot, there is often a hidden, subterranean life where the characters unconsciously act out ancient patterns of classic legends and mythologies, thereby bearing witness to Jung's theories on the collective unconscious and its archetypes.

In an introductory chapter, the views of the artist on Latin American literature, its distinctive features and role, are set forth.

Preface

MIGUEL ANGEL ASTURIAS of Guatemala received the Nobel Prize for literature in 1967. Until then, only two or three articles about him had ever appeared in English, although he was widely acknowledged as one of the leading novelists of the Spanish-speaking world. The recognition he had also received in France and in other European nations contrasts with most of the English world's perplexity when his name was announced by the Swedish Academy. Nevertheless, his reading public here will grow when the projected translation of his books is ready, and I hope this study will contribute to a fuller enjoyment of them.

Among those who already know Asturias, there are some who see in his works on political and social dictatorship the finest novels of protest we have. For others, his fanciful tales of Indian and Spanish folklore, told in the rich and ambiguous language of dreamwork, have the inexhaustible value of poetry. The quality of his writing in both these fields has sufficed to establish his reputation; but I have discovered that his invention and craftsmanship are controlled by an overall design: much of his work is built on the depth psychology of Carl G. Jung or, more exactly, on the evolution of consciousness revealed by Jungian analysis of the primordial images or archetypes found in myths. Just as the process of this growth moves through definite stages but remains for the most part unperceived, so does the corresponding process in Asturias' books. Therefore, in addition to acquainting English speaking readers with the author's works and ideas, I have endeavored to outline this substructure of meaning when feasible, for without an awareness of it, no evaluation of his achievements could be made.

In the judgment of the late Mexican critic Alfonso Reyes, Asturias has written good poetry all through life, but I have confined myself to his prose, partly owing to space limitations. When referring to Maya Indian writings I have used the translations of Georges Raynaud, although they have not been rendered into English, because Asturias considers them to be closest to the originals, and they are the ones he uses.

All translations from Asturias are my own. Some of the material in this book has appeared in modified form in *Hispania*, *Cuadernos Hispanoamericanos*, *Hispanic Review*, and *Reseña*.

I am indebted to Editorial Losada, Buenos Aires, for permission to quote from Asturias' works; I am also grateful to *Atlas* magazine for allowing me to use excerpts from an interview granted by Asturias to Günter W. Lorenz, and to Istituto Editoriale Cisalpino for letting me quote from Giuseppe Bellini, *La narrativa di Miguel Ángel Asturias*.

R.J.C.

University of New Hampshire

ABOUT THE AUTHOR

Richard Callan is associate professor of Spanish American literature at the University of New Hampshire. He fell under the spell of Asturias' story-telling magic at first reading and soon discovered that there was even more delight to be had from *re*-reading him. As his addiction to Asturias' books developed, he found himself driven by them to explore other fields such as comparative religion, anthropology, analytical psychology, and consequently came to look upon Asturias as an effective teacher of culture and self-knowledge.

He was born in New York (1932) and has published articles on literary subjects in various journals.

Contents

Preface

Chronology

1. Asturias, the Man 11

2. *El Señor Presidente* 18

3. Babylonian Mythology in *El Señor Presidente* 33

4. *Hombres de maíz* 53

5. The Quest for the Feminine 71

6. *Viento fuerte* 85

7. *El Papa Verde* 97

8. *Los ojos de los enterrados* 112

9. His Five Dramas 120

10. Short Stories 152

    Epilogue 161

    Notes and References 167

    Selected Bibliography 175

    Index 179

MIGUEL ANGEL ASTURIAS

Chronology

1899   Miguel Angel Asturias born October 19, Guatemala City, of Ernesto Asturias and María Rosales.

1905   Moves to the farm of his paternal grandparents at Salamá, Baja Verapaz.

1908   Returns to Guatemala to live in Parroquia Vieja suburb.

1922   Helps found La Universidad Popular de Guatemala which operates successfully with branches in the provinces until President Ubico closes it in 1932.

1923   Law degree. Dissertation: "The Social Problem of the Indian" awarded the Gálvez Prize. To Europe for political safety and to further his education.

1928   Short visit to Guatemala. Publishes *La arquitectura de la vida nueva*, four lectures given during this visit.

1930   *Leyendas de Guatemala* (Madrid).

1932   Awarded Sylla Monségur Prize for the French translation of *Leyendas de Guatemala*.

1933   Returns to Guatemala via New York.

1945   Sent to Mexico as cultural attaché by revolutionary government of Juan José Arévalo.

1946   *El Señor Presidente* privately published in Mexico.

1947   Cultural attaché to Buenos Aires until 1953.

1949   *Sien de alondra*, anthology of his poetry, and *Hombres de maíz*.

1950   *Viento fuerte*.

1953   Named Ambassador to El Salvador in October by President Arbenz.

1954   Deprived of citizenship by Colonel Castillo Armas. Exile to South America. *El papa verde*.

1955   *Soluna*.

1956   *Week-end en Guatemala*, dedicated to Blanca, his wife.

1957   *La audiencia de los confines.*

1959   Passport returned by President Ydígoras Fuentes at the insistence of University of Guatemala.

1960   *Los ojos de los enterrados.*

1961   *El alhajadito.*

1962   To Italy from Buenos Aires after fall of President Arturo Frondizi. Travels through Rumania.

1963   *El Señor Presidente* published in London, first book translated into English (same version published in New York 1964). *Mulata de tal.*

1964   *Rumania: su nueva imagen,* a large format travel book, and *Teatro* (four plays).

1965   *Clarivigilia primaveral,* a cycle of poems on how the Maya gods created the artist.

1966   Awarded Lenin Peace Prize. Named Ambassador to France by President Méndez Montenegro, moderate leftist.

1967   Nobel Prize for Literature October 19, his sixty-eighth birthday. *El espejo de Lida Sal* in Paris and Mexico. English translation of *Mulata de tal* published in Boston.

1968   *Latinoamérica y otros ensayos,* a collection of fourteen essays.

1969   *Maladrón.*

CHAPTER 1

Asturias, the Man

I *His Life*: "*Keep on learning all through life*"

MIGUEL ANGEL ASTURIAS, the son of a magistrate and a schoolteacher, was born in Guatemala in 1899, a year after the accession of President Estrada Cabrera. Because Asturias' father could not get along with the dictator, he had to retire from his practice and move with his family to the country. In 1908 they returned to the outskirts of the city where Asturias spent his adolescence. Life in the metropolis was transformed, he writes, by the great earthquakes of 1917 and 1918, because the people who had lived withdrawn in their homes, apprehensive and distrustful of their neighbors out of dread of the regime, were forced to move into tents and communal living quarters. From this renewed human contact, a spirit of solidarity emerged that led to the overthrow of the president in 1920. In 1922, Asturias and other students founded the Popular University, a community project whereby the middle class was encouraged to contribute to the general welfare by teaching free courses to the underprivileged.

Asturias obtained his law degree in 1923 with a thesis on Indian problems, for which he received the Gálvez Prize. That year he left for Europe, where he lived for ten years. In 1928 he returned for a visit during which he addressed the Popular University. The aim of the university, he told the students, mostly laborers, was to teach them to be free, free from the slavery of ignorance, drunkenness, and sexuality, and to help them attain these freedoms through exercise of their will. Students were also taught to be useful, he continued, by learning to respect all forms of life and the value of time. "Let us keep on learning all through life, ever searching for more light."[1] He also lectured at a boys' preparatory school, comparing life to an architectural structure: the bright upstairs, the zone of ideas; the ground floor, darker, the zone of feelings; and the cellar, the storeroom of the unconscious. He proceeded to show the youths how to construct their lives in these three areas, emphasizing the importance of conjugal love and the influence of the unconscious, two subjects to be pursued at length in his novels.

Asturias first stayed in London, frequenting the British Museum's Maya Indian collection, but he soon moved to Paris. He enrolled at the Sorbonne to study Central American anthropology and mythology under Professor Georges Raynaud, a scholar who devoted forty years to translating the *Popol Vuh*, according to Asturias. With another student Asturias translated Raynaud's French version of it into Spanish in 1927, and the following year they did the same with Raynaud's version of the *Annals of the Cakchiquels*. In the course of his ten years in France Asturias took many trips abroad, particularly to Greece, Egypt, and the Near East. He also took part in the Surrealist movement of the 1920's. In 1933 he went back to live in Guatemala, remaining there throughout the administration of another dictator, Ubico. He founded and managed the radio news program, "Diario del Aire," mentioned in *Los ojos de los enterrados*, a novel depicting that period. Ubico was overthrown in 1944, and under the democratic government of President Arévalo, Asturias entered the diplomatic corps, serving nine years in Mexico, Buenos Aires, and El Salvador. In 1946 he privately published his first novel, *El Señor Presidente*, written over a ten-year period (1922–32) but kept in a drawer for fourteen years because of the foul political situation.

A new dictatorship, established in 1954, deprived Asturias of his passport and citizenship, and forced him into exile. In 1955 he stayed with the poet Pablo Neruda in Chile, later moving to Buenos Aires; but Argentine politics took a backward step in 1962 and he went to live in Genoa. In 1966 the new president of Guatemala, Julio César Méndez Montenegro, appointed him ambassador to France, the post he presently holds. That year he was awarded the Lenin Peace Prize, and the following year he received the Nobel Prize for Literature— the first Latin American novelist to do so. He has traveled widely throughout Europe, Asia, and America. He is married to Blanca Mora Araujo of Argentina. A biography by his friend Günter W. Lorenz is said to be forthcoming.

II *Views on Latin American Literature*

More useful for an understanding of the literary output of Asturias than the scant facts of his life are his views on Latin American literature, past and future. In lectures and interviews Asturias has pointed out its distinguishing features. It is primarily a literature of protest: beginning with the Conquistadors, a compulsion to dispute misjudgments, to correct injustices, and to remonstrate against the excesses of exploitation that plagued the continent then as now, drove the men of the New World to register their dissension in books, letters and chronicles. Predating any of these, however, the writings of the Indians themselves are the headwaters of all social protest in America. In documents such as the Maya books of *Chilam Balam*, the original inhabitants of the continent expressed their reaction to the barbarity of the Conquest.

The need for expostulation continued down the centuries as one form of abuse succeeded another. The main streams of protest literature were political and social or "Indianist." In the twentieth century a third source of rancor developed from the exploitation of natural resources by corporations from abroad: oil wells, mines, plantations; their economic dictatorship led to what Asturias terms the "democratic enslavement" of native farmers and workers. The literature of protest deriving from the various conflicts is far from being tractarian. On the contrary, the most successful novels of this type are dispassionate testimonies of reality in which the style is objective and the situations speak for themselves. This is the strength of works by novelists like Ciro Alegría and Rómulo Gallegos.

Asturias feels that the most serious threat to fiction today is its drift toward journalism, the reporting of factual events laced with a plot to give it the name of fiction. In this century of civilized barbarism, he explains, documented facts can easily outdo anything a novelist might create. Fictional episodes may seem paler than actual experiences, and the strength of the latter's authority impresses them on literal minds; but whatever documentary fiction may gain in actuality, it loses in permanency and usually falls outside the field of literature. This is an important issue with Asturias, essential for an appreciation of his novels. Several of these are laid in recognizable periods of Guatemalan history, and his situations occasionally recall actual ones. Nevertheless, the events he narrates are entirely fictitious, and readers are sometimes disconcerted to find that his novels are in no sense historical. Leaving facts to history, he creates a parallel world with its own events and people and borrows from actuality only the spirit of the times, which he often personifies in a created character. A case in point is *El papa verde* (The Green Pope), the second volume of his Banana Trilogy. In the protagonist, the American adventurer who promotes the banana company, bringing it and himself to a position of absolute power, Asturias has created a personality with far more vitality than any individual known to United Fruit could possess, a man who epitomizes the enterprising spirit of that monopoly in all its genius and ruthlessness.

Contemporary European trends such as the literature of the absurd, of futility and boredom, have little place in America, to Asturias' way of thinking; there is still too much to be accomplished, too many rights to be realized, too many needs to be filled and nations to be built. He feels that the task of the writer in America is to be a guide and a prophet; not to take sides or to extol one faction over another, but to throw light on the problems of the continent. Participation in social and political concerns partakes of a moral obligation for most of them, and, with the exception of a short period of estheticism at the turn of the century, this has been the trend throughout the history of Spanish American literature. Personal involvement can therefore be considered one of its features, a corollary of protest literature. Ideally, the novel of protest is therefore neither strident nor journalistic, nor does it try to promote or to prove anything. The point Asturias insists upon is that it can and must be a work of art; he is adamant in this matter, and his own works show that it can be done.

Another characteristic that distinguishes the Latin American novel from others is its treatment of setting. To read one of these works, Asturias points out, is to penetrate into a fundamentally different world from that of a European novel, where nature generally has little more than a decorative value. In the Old World nature has long been dominated, whereas in America it is still a force superior to man, and its effect on his behavior and character is inescapable. In novels that reflect this fact, nature can no longer function as a backdrop Instead, it assumes a positive role of its own, often becoming the moving principle of the plot or acting as the protagonist. An example may be found in José Eustasio Rivera's *La vorágine* (*The Vortex*) where men who slave in Brazilian backlands gathering rubber think of the jungle as a sentient monster that will take revenge on them if they offend her. In the religion of the American aborigines, the elements and the vegetation are systematically deified; it is necessary for men to personify the inscrutable forces of nature in this way in order to cope with them mentally—as did the Greeks, for instance. This is one of the reasons, no doubt, why Asturias links his novels with the religions of early man; the pre-eminence of nature is still indisputable in most of this continent. In many novels nature intervenes forcefully as the living reality that molds and controls the human characters for better or for worse, transforming them either into giants or into beasts. In the view of Asturias and many of his colleagues, man is indissolubly bound to the earth and cannot be seen in isolation from it. It is this unifying vision of man and nature that characterizes the Latin American novel and furnishes a basis for its universality. We shall see that this link with the forces of nature which primitive people have preserved is, from the viewpoint of psychology, an advantage they have over the civilized.

Finally, there is the matter of form. Asturias says that one of the major concerns of the modern novel in Spanish America is language. Less staid than European literature, with no tradition to follow or to break, each literary undertaking in the New World is a linguistic adventure, as the author adapts his words to the world he is creating. Today's experiments with multiple images and sound patterns are often inspired by the ways of expression peculiar to the ancient peoples of America. To them words were above all sacred, dedicated to the gods. In Maya cosmogony man was created to speak to the gods, and the first creatures were failures because the gods could not understand them. Words also had a divine power because, being echoic, to pronounce a word correctly was to create that which was named, or to possess mastery of it. Earth! said the gods, and the earth came into being. Words were magic formulas containing the essence of things.

Writing in modern Spanish, Latin American authors attempt to recapture the lost echoic values of words by other methods, chiefly through onomatopoeia. Asturias employs this poetic device as a means of verbally depicting the sounds of his country; the most celebrated example is the opening paragraph of *El Señor Presidente* where the sinister ringing of cathedral bells, reproduced by the rhythmic repetition of ominous U—UM sounds, foreshadows the hellish horrors in the dictator's domains. This and many selections from his works should be read aloud for best effect, in much the same way as poetry. Indeed, Asturias is of the opinion that the best novels of Latin America seem not to be written so much as spoken, and that their originality lies in the successful transposition of reality into a world of images, where words, expressing concept *and* sound, function magically.

Another feature drawn from Indian stylistics, parallelism (a kind of antiphony), is expressed in modern novels by double and triple metaphors. Through such multiple images the novelist conveys the thoughts and feelings of his characters and his own, so that some novels appear to be composed in a language of images rather than words. Puns and double meanings were also highly appreciated by the Indians, which led them to figurative language and to any form of ambiguity that enriched the texture of narrative. To express themselves at all in their ideograms they had to be poets and find symbols that would suggest ideas and feelings. Obviously, rhetorical maneuvers like these held a special appeal to the Surrealist in Asturias, and he utilized them to great advantage in conveying the various levels on which his novels may be understood. This is the language of poetry, and the resulting poetic prose, like much modern poetry, throws the burden of interpretation on the reader. To Asturias, America is a world of magical realism which can only be expressed in the poetic key.

The blending of social, political, and poetic elements is peculiar to Latin American literature, and probably not found elsewhere. The factor common to the three characteristics Asturias describes is a desire to portray the continent, which is ultimately the constant protagonist of all the novels, whether they are exploring new verbal possibilities in order to portray her, recapturing the voices of her landscapes and climates, or protesting abuses against her.

Asturias feels that instead of adopting European models and writing to please European tastes, as some do, Latin American writers and poets must use their talents to produce the works that will best express this New World, not out of chauvinism, but in order to create a distinctive and authentically American literature.[2] Just how far all his ideas apply to the works of the other writers is not our purpose to determine, but they serve as an excellent outline of his own designs and accomplishments.

CHAPTER 2

El Señor Presidente

ASTURIAS' first novel, *El Señor Presidente*, has always been the public's favorite because, though laid in 1916, its subject—dictatorship—continues to be of burning actuality. Its most obvious purpose is to show the excesses to which power in the hands of one man can lead. There are several less evident meanings to the book, as will be shown, but the plot of political protest has engrossed most readers. It is a stirring novel with great artistic qualities of style and technique.

The narrative structure of *El Señor Presidente* is extremely complex, and even the details of the action can only be mastered in retrospect, after the book has been carefully read and analyzed. Most of the novel is either presented dramatically or narrated through the perceptions of the characters, in the manner of speech peculiar to their age, class, and sex, and since lies, insinuations, surmises, and misinformation are the stuff that dictatorships are made of, they also prevail in the novel; it is up to the reader to disentangle the truth from conflicting reports and to reconstruct the plot for himself.

The story opens with the accidental murder of a high official, Colonel Parrales Sonriente, by an idiot whom the officer has awakened by shouting "Mother!" in his ear. The idiot, ordinarily harmless, leaps up, chokes the officer to death, then runs off aimlessly into the night, unaware of his deed. This occurs Monday night. The President uses the Colonel's death to dispose of two men, Carvajal and General Canales, about whom he has received slanderous reports, by pinning the murder on them. Carvajal, a lawyer, will be arrested, sentenced by a kangaroo court, and shot. As for Canales, in order to make him appear guilty, the dictator plans to have him shot while fleeing. He has the General's house surrounded by detectives who are to shoot him if he attempts to escape and tells the Chief of Police to arrest him Thursday morning. On Wednesday he directs his favorite, Don Miguel Cara de Angel, to persuade Canales at all costs to leave town that night, explaining that for state reasons Canales must not be jailed but that the police must know nothing about it.

Such are the President's tactics, which are not stated outright, but must be inferred from the action. His scheme against Canales foreshadows a far more sadistic one against Cara de Angel. His word is law; nobody questions it, not even mentally. If he decides that Canales and Carvajal are guilty, the arm of justice has only to punish them. When the Chief of Police interrogates witnesses, he tortures them until they tell the "truth" as the President dictated it, and this is the only evidence he records.

Cara de Angel is pleased to be entrusted with saving a man's life, a change from his usual nefarious duties. The favorite is an elegant young bachelor on whose unquestioning service the dictator has often relied. He contacts General Canales and convinces him that his immediate flight is imperative. They agree on a plan whereby thugs are to break into the General's home at 2 A.M. to distract the police. During the confusion the General is to make his escape through the back while Cara de Angel is to escort Canales' daughter to one of her uncles. In hiring the thugs, however, the favorite pretends that he is in love with the Canales girl and wants to abduct her. He knows that nobody, not even the thugs, would expose themselves to any political involvement, whereas for assault and robbery there is no danger of punishment.

All goes off as Don Miguel plans, and the General gets away safely. The President's scheme of having him shot while fleeing misfires simply because the police rush in behind the burglars to see what they can loot. Indeed, one of the burglars, Vásquez, a policeman off duty, assured Miguel that this would happen. The General struggles through the mountains. First he is befriended by a homeless Indian who has been defrauded of his land by the government. Then he stays with some country relatives who tell him another sad tale of suffering at the hands of officials. To learn that so many criminals are protected by the dictator bolsters the old gentleman's resolve to return and free the country by revolution. He gathers a handful of dispossessed Indians who are willing to follow him, but while still hiding in the mountains he dies of a heart attack. This has been interpreted to mean that Asturias wants no more revolutions led by army men.

Meanwhile, uncounted complications have arisen. The uncles of the Canales girl refuse to take her lest they be compromised. She becomes deathly ill, and while looking after her, Miguel falls in love with her. When she is about to die he marries her, but she recovers, and after a short idyll they are separated forever; Miguel goes to prison where he dies after many years. But this section is the core of the book and we will come back to it. During that same Wednesday night a certain Fedina Rodas hears that there is a plot to abduct Camila Canales. As Miss Camila is to be the godmother of her baby son, she runs over to warn her Thursday at dawn, but she finds only the maid who is dying and the wreckage of a beautiful home. The Chief of Police, who has come to arrest Canales, seizes her as an accomplice. Questioned concerning the General's whereabouts, she can tell nothing, so she is tortured. They make her grind quicklime while listening to her baby cry from hunger in the next room. When she faints she is thrown back in her cell with the infant. It dies, and she spends the next day in shock, clutching the tiny corpse, under the impression that it has returned into her body. Meanwhile the madam of a brothel "buys" her from the Chief of Police. At the brothel the girls discover the shriveled body which has begun to smell; they organize a wake that turns into an orgy as each prostitute weeps over the dead baby, mourning the son she never had.

Occasionally the scene shifts from the harrowing action to a prison cell where three men are being held who are not connected with any other characters: a sacristan, a student, and a schoolteacher. Whereas everyone else is engrossed in his own affairs, the student and the teacher worry about the state of the nation; this torments them more than their own plight. The older man thinks the country has been reduced to a wasteland for which there is no hope, but before dying he takes comfort from the student's awareness of it and from hearing him react against those who preach resignation.

The President of the title rarely appears in the novel but he is the efficient cause of most of the action. The moving love story of the protagonist, Miguel Cara de Angel, provides the only conflict that escapes the dictator's control for a short while. The book has been called a study of fear because fear is the climate in which it unfolds.[1] Fear is a weapon that the President wields with skill but against which he himself is defenseless; fear strikes high and low; it grips the cruel and the brave and reduces each in turn to the standing of a rag doll—all but one. Ironically, that one is physically the most grotesque and puppet-like of all; he is a legless, blind beggar who is swung and thrown around like a beanbag by a policeman. But he refuses to testify to a lie because, he says, it would be unmanly; enraged, the Chief of Police takes it as a personal slur and has him beaten to death.

The novel has also been called a study in time for time is the true protagonist of a dictatorship. Endless as time feels to the victims, it is their only hope; conversely, for the dictator, time is a constant threat to his power and place. In his work Asturias has experimented with great success in rendering perceptual or psychological time through the medium of words, contracting and expanding duration according to the joys or anguishes he wishes to depict.[2]

I   *The Metaphysical Conflict*

Despite its political overtones, however, *El Señor Presidente* is not intrinsically a political novel. The understandable assumption that it is persists, diverting many readers' attention from the essence of the book and from the protagonist's emotional evolution. If we are restricted to a political understanding of the plot, the outcome is perplexing and the fate that befalls Cara de Angel is pointless; whereas, if we seek an explanation on another level, namely, in the old pagan and medieval theme of fertility, we will find that the plot unravels satisfactorily.

In a proper political novel the main character would be

expected to have some opinion about the government or about the manner in which the chief of state discharges his duties; but with Cara de Angel, no political thought ever enters his mind; consequently there is no development in that direction. His relations with the President are purely personal and remain so to the last: "What luck to get away from that man!" he tells himself on his way out of the country.[3] It is the man, not the dictator, that he resents, and if on one occasion he feels like murdering the man, it is only over a private grievance.

True, minor characters harbor a feeling of rebellion but it leads to nothing. The idea of an uprising never occurred to General Canales until after the dictator had unjustly turned against him. Even so, he organized his little band of Indians to recoup his dignity after an unsoldierly flight and on second thought as a political move. Nobody ever gets anything done, as the President complains: "This nation is made up of 'going' people. . . . 'I'm going to do this, I'm going to do that' but for lack of determination they neither do or undo anything" (p. 268). Indeed, the political inertia of the entire population is a necessary setting to make credible the fabulous atrocities of the government. Even the student's cry: "Why are you praying? This is no time for prayers! Let's break down this door and start a revolution!" uttered as it is in a prison cell remains inoperative (p. 212). Once freed, the youth simply returns to the blind alley where he lives. Along the way he sees, outlined against an azure sky, a demented dwarf mounted on a broom and charging over little volcanoes of dust and rubble. This is a bitter travesty of the city's emblem and a commentary on what the dictator's rule has done to the nation. The dust and rubble are tokens of the dictator's insane destructiveness; here they recall the volcanoes of Guatemala, and the scene parodies the escutcheon of Santiago de los Caballeros de Guatemala where the city's patron, Saint James, is seen galloping over the national volcanoes.

The conflict in which Miguel Cara de Angel is immersed unfolds entirely outside the realm of politics. He enters the novel as the President's favorite, and before the end he has become the victim of the tyrant's most studied brutality and murder, although he never lifts a finger or utters a word to harm the man, has no intention of doing so, and the President knows it. There can be no explanation for this other than an emotional or subconscious one.

Miguel does undergo a change although it does not alter his outward submission to the dictator. He falls in love against his will, against his judgment, and the transfiguring power that this unprecedented experience, love, has upon him is the core of the book. It is a slow process, not by calendar count perhaps, but in perceptual time. He becomes engrossed in Camila to the exclusion of everything else. Can the President be said to become jealous? Yes, in a sense, for he cannot suffer anything less than absolute ascendancy over the person of his favorite. In addition to the psychological factor, the enmity that Miguel's evolution engenders in the President is based on the archetypal contest between fertility and destruction, the President embodying sterility and death while his favorite moves steadily into a position where he impersonates the generative forces of nature. The theme of this cyclic struggle provides a key to the meaning of *El Señor Presidente*.

The plausibility of a moral transformation in such a man as Miguel, the favorite tool of an inhuman dictator, rests largely on a kind of rectitude which guided him in the Canales affair. After he has conceived and worked out the plan of escape for the General he feels that his service will give him a right over the General's daughter as soon as the man gets away safely. Later, when he realizes that the President's full intention is to have the General shot while fleeing, Miguel's frustration is not only over the use to which he is being put, but also over losing the girl, because according to his private code of conduct, if he leads her father into a deathtrap, his right to possess her will be lost. This slim trace of self–discipline paves the way for his subsequent behavior toward her.

After a taste of constructive action in preparing the General's flight, it suits him ill to be jolted back into his customary role of a mindless instrument of death in the hands of the President. The uneasiness he feels is an existential thirst for something other than the wasteland and static existence he has known. At the prompting of this new thirst, he decides to obey the letter of the President's command and to counter what he now knows to be its spirit, thus opening a mental breach for the first time between himself and the tyrant.

After Canales has made his escape and Camila has been abducted, Don Miguel sits with her in the back room of a cantina across the street. As he waits for her to stop crying, he begins to feel sorry for her, and instead of carrying out his design he comforts her with a fatherly pat. He is falling in love with her, of course. His resistance to this process is manifested by the relief which tempers his regret after what he thinks is a final separation from her. They are immediately thrown together again, however, by Camila's pneumonia. She is stricken in the back room of the bar where she was hiding, homeless and rejected by her relatives, her reputation ruined by her compromising situation. The tavern owner, La Masacuata, becomes her nurse, and Miguel will be at her side day and night. The example of her helplessness will lead him to discover his inner self.

II *"Love is Strong as Death . . ."*

Camila's condition deteriorates rapidly, and when the doctor gives up hope for her recovery, Cara de Angel conceives the idea of performing a good deed in order to win a miracle from God. The good deed consists in saving the life of a certain Mayor Farfán by secretly warning him of an order from the President to give him an overdose of sedative the next time he is intoxicated. For the second time Miguel deflects one of the tyrant's deathblows, explaining that he is offering Farfán's life in exchange for Camila's. In reality it is his own life that he is exchanging for hers: Farfán is a garrulous drunkard who is sure to divulge the story of Miguel's warning, which is sure to be reported to the authorities. Cara de Angel foresees this, at least subconsciously, as we know from the dream he has immediately following his conversation with Farfán. In his dream he sees the Chief of Police, his sworn enemy, joyously brandishing an anonymous letter which is undoubtedly the letter of denunciation. It must be this act of love and folly followed by his marriage *in extremis*, that brings upon him the tyrant's deadly wrath, because by it Miguel betrays his total change of heart.

It is a measure of Miguel's love to have subordinated his welfare to Camila's. The miracle of her recovery will be no greater than the miracle that led him, a heartless man, to commit himself unconditionally to another person. So dependent upon her has he become that without her the world no longer has meaning. He begins to realize that man in the absolute, as he is when he stands alone and without reference to anything or anyone, is unproductive nothingness, but that if he will accept a relative position, if he will adopt an attitude of dependence upon another being, he can triumph over sterility and extinction. United to woman, man's being is completed and his life can become creative. Cara de Angel learns and suffers this truth in his own flesh and spirit during Camila's illness. Just as she is utterly dependent on others, he becomes dependent upon her as a result of the strange power of love, a humbling but not humiliating experience. The barrenness of self-sufficiency is thus contrasted with the fruitful giving of self. It is a constant theme with Asturias, recurring in its many forms throughout his works and in the practice of his own life.

To be helpful, a neighbor of La Masacuata holds a consultation with a theosophist, spiritist, and dabbler in occult sciences nicknamed Tícher because he teaches English. Upon hearing the tale of the dying girl and her devoted suitor, Tícher recommends marriage as a cure: love can contend with death, he reasons, because it is as strong as death. Therefore, by committing an act of love, which marriage is, Miguel can overcome death and save her: "Only love can oppose death because both are equally strong, as it says in the Song of Songs." Miguel follows the advice, the marriage takes place at once, and after the ceremony Tícher exclaims in English: "Make thee another self, for love of me!" (p. 223).

The key line of the fertility theme is Tícher's dictum: "Only love can oppose death" ("A la muerte únicamente se le puede oponer el amor"). It establishes the poles of opposition between the President's stance and the position toward which Miguel has been moving since his first rebellious impulse when he prevented the murder of Canales. Tícher then indicates the means by which love overcomes death: "Make thee another self. . ." It is a quotation from Sonnet X, one of Shakespeare's progeny sonnets where he presses "W. H." to marry, to beget children, and to defy death by living on in them.

How to overcome the President? As a political question there is no answer to be found here, but if we modify the wording and ask how to overcome death and destruction as personified in the President, the novel responds: through love, because love leads to new life, to fertility. "For love is strong as death" (Song of Songs 8:6). In a sense, *El Señor Presidente* can be considered an extended commentary on this passage from the Bible.

If the detailed progress of Miguel's spiritual refinement is not always immediately apparent to the reader, one of the reasons is because Asturias employs Surrealistic devices to present the inner life of his characters, making demands upon the reader's creative imagination to forward the action. As his techniques were then uncommon (the novel was written between 1922 and 1932), Asturias took the trouble to point out and exemplify how the reader should go about interpreting him. In the last chapter but one, Camila, the bride of Don Miguel, is pregnant, and she has not heard from him since he left for Washington months before. She dreams that she is lying in a hammock sucking a caramel and playing with a rubber ball. The ball slips from her hands and bounces away until it vanishes, while the caramel grows and grows until it fills her mouth. Asturias gives us to understand that the disappearing ball stands for her husband, who will fade out of her life, and the caramel for her son who will soon fill it, in the following words: "But her husband had run to fetch the ball. Now she remembered that part of her dream. The big patio. The little black ball. Her husband getting smaller and smaller, further and further away, as if reduced by a lens, until he disappeared right out of the patio after the ball, while in her mouth (and she wasn't thinking of her son) the caramel was growing bigger" (p. 287). In this way, Asturias authorizes us to interpret other ambiguous passages of his book.

When the report of Miguel's marriage reaches the President,

his reaction is hostile, but for appearances he orders the wedding to be announced as a social event over which he presided. The ensuing interview between the two, however, shows that the dictator has instinctively recognized the extent of his favorite's alienation. Thoroughly intoxicated, he betrays that what irks him is not *whom* Miguel married (the daughter of an enemy), but *how.* "*In articulo mortis...* at the point of death," he keeps repeating with loud guffaws (p. 232). The fact that it was an uncalculated act of love, this is what the President intuits and cannot tolerate. The man who was his tool has suddenly assumed a life of its own, and exhibits a character fundamentally antipathetic to him, besides.

Taken by surprise by the dictator's coarse mockery, Don Miguel is seized with murderous rage, but he quickly manages to control it—as he notes with profound self-contempt. In his state of anguish and shock he does not fathom the depth of the presidential enmity, nor does he sense the threat behind the game of patience the tyrant ironically describes, the fly game. Who more likely than he, though, to play the fly to the President's spider?

III   *"Make Thee Another Self. . . ."*

Watching over Camila's convalescence, Cara de Angel is conscious of being swept along by a mysterious fate that controls him. United though they are now, he feels estranged from her by the very fact of their marriage, to which neither of them had wholly consented. Much as he desires Camila, his love craves nothing less than the ideal of mutual passion. As for Camila, her uneasiness over this matter is described indirectly by a technique peculiar to Asturias through which he portrays his characters' subconscious preoccupations by a subjective treatment of setting. The device is particularly suited to portray the bewilderment of a girl who has revived from a bout with death to find herself bereft of family and home and married to a near stranger. She takes a walk into the country with her husband and stops to watch coffee pickers whose hands move about the branches like hungry animals: "rising, dropping, coming together crazily as if tickling the

tree, then darting away as if pulling off its shirt" (p. 248).
The similes which the fluttering hands suggest to her illustrate
apprehensions of which she may not be fully aware—this is
what she expected that Miguel's hands would do to her.

The two go for a dip in a swimming pool and as the day
ends the groom who brings up their horses offers Camila some
fresh eggs, thinking she might be hungry: "No, I don't like
them raw, and they might hurt me," she answers. "You see
I've just got up from a sickbed" (p. 251). Eggs symbolize the
act of love; mention of their rawness suggests unreciprocated
desire. In this Surrealistic manner she justifies to herself
Miguel's singular postponement of his conjugal rights, saying
in effect, No, not just now; it is too soon after my illness and
might do me harm. Whereupon the peasant rejoins: " 'But
now you'll soon be well again! ... Women are like flowers,
they need to be watered; marriage will put you back on your
feet!' Camila lowered her eyes, blushing, startled... but first
she looked at her husband and they desired each other with a
glance, sealing the tacit agreement that had been missing
between them" (p. 251).

These words are the climax of the fertility theme: "They
desired each other" ("Se desearon"). Just as Tícher's dictum
"Only love can oppose death" was the key line that epitomized
the plot, this is the key moment toward which Cara de Angel
has been straining instinctively and inevitably throughout
his journey from the basest to the purest expression of passion,
the flowering of conjugal love. From this crucial point in the
fertility cycle, the narrative hurries toward the inevitably
tragic outcome.

During his last encounter with the President, Cara de Angel
glances out the window and beholds a re-enactment of the
Maya Quiché myth wherein the rain god Tohil demands
human sacrifice.[4] The tribes acquiesce: "And the tribes brought
into his presence their best hunters, those with the erect blowguns, those with the ever-loaded slings..." (p. 272).

The scene serves to equate the President with the cruel
god, and Miguel with the hunters about to be sacrificed.
Were he of a mind to intepret it, it would notify him of his
own impending immolation and bring to his awareness the

battle in which he is engaged. Just as he confronts the President, the two mythical contenders stand face to face: the
hunters, whose erect blowguns and loaded slingshots are the
ever-fertile organs of human reproduction, and the bloodthirsty Tohil-President, whose object is to destroy. Don
Miguel does sense some danger, however, and as a means of
escape he seizes joyfully upon the mission abroad with which
the chief of state pretends to entrust him. Once out of the
country, he plans to go into hiding with Camila and live
quietly on his fortune, with no thought, significantly, of plotting
or agitating, or doing anything for his stricken land.

This desire to escape is novel for him. In the early part of
the story he expressed contrary views on the subject. He had
been talking with a woodsman who took him for an angel
because of his physical beauty and the way he had suddenly
appeared in the twilight. The peasant's first thought was to
ingratiate himself with the "angel" by a display of Christian
resignation. He was a poor man, he explained, but satisfied
with his lot—not like some people who were always wanting
impossible things. His wife, for instance, wished she had
wings:

> "So your wife would like to have wings on Sundays?" said the
> apparition. "Even if she had them, they'd be of no use to her."
> "That's right; although she says she wants them to go for a
> stroll." "Her own two feet are good enough for that. Even if she
> had wings, she wouldn't go anywhere." "Certainly not...because
> a woman is a bird that can't get along without its cage." (p. 30)

Obviously here Don Miguel is not particularly interested in
wings or in flying, symbols of freedom. It is the closest he comes
to making a political statement anywhere in the book. Freedom
is worthless, he seems to feel. Why yearn for impossible things?
Even if the door of their cage were opened, people would only
cower and cling to the bars. Although Miguel's cage is larger
than the Indian's, he is in one too, and he does not feel that
freedom would mean anything to him. He and the woodsman
are agreed on this, as are the two classes they represent. The
peasant declares himself satisfied with his lot in order to impress
his angel favorably: it is possible, he tells himself hopefully

that the angel will reward his Christian attitude by making
him a king. He pictures himself dressed in gold and crimson,
with crown and scepter. The President is Don Miguel's "angel,"
for is he not currying the President's favor in order to receive
his gold and crimson bonanza? This is the spirit that makes
tyranny possible, the frame of mind that leads men to await
from above, from heaven or from superiors, that which heaven
will not give and which man grants at too high a price. It is
the pernicious hope that chance may single them out as in a
lottery.

The farewell embrace of Miguel and Camila is sketched
simultaneously with the frantic flight of a chicken pursued and
killed by a kitchenmaid in the patio: "The chicken ran into the
wall, or the wall came down upon him. He felt both things
happening to him in his heart" (p. 275). By alternating the
sentences which describe these two incidents, the end of one
life, the beginning of another,[5] Asturias illustrates the unending
birth-death-rebirth cycle as well as the parallel which exists
between the two actions. The chicken's motions can substitute
for Miguel's and vice versa because death spasms correspond
inscrutably to the transport of passion.

If the dying chicken is a figure for Miguel today, it is a
premonitory one for him as he will be tomorrow. Don Miguel
completes the first lap of his trip confidently, but upon arriving
at the port of embarkation he is arrested, thrown in a boxcar
and thrashed with a whip, while another man assumes his
identity and sails in his place. Like the chicken, Cara de Angel
crashes against a wall. He has come to have second thoughts
about wings and freedom: "Tears blinded him. He wanted to
break down the doors, to flee, to run, to fly, to cross the sea,
not be the one who was staying behind" (p. 279).

The official making the arrest is Mayor Farfán, the one
Miguel had saved. The President seems to have pardoned him
and specially selected him for this job to make his favorite's
disappointment doubly bitter. The venom Farfán puts into
beating his prisoner betrays a recognition of his own abjection.
He is further goaded by the oddly triumphant cry of Miguel:
"Go on, strike, don't be afraid; this is what I am a man for,
and your whip is the weapon of the impotent" (*castrados*)

(p. 282). This taunt, on the surface a commonplace insult, must not be taken as a banality in this context. It is reminiscent of the blind man's jeer about lies being unmanly that infuriated the Chief of Police. The gibe touches Farfán because he consorts only with harlots (figures of sterility for the purpose of this novel), and it reaches beyond him to hit the President whom he represents. It is Cara de Angel's moment of triumph, ironically, because at this point he is the very embodiment of the life forces which ultimately frustrate the President and render him impotent. Compulsively, the tyrant strikes at him, but he strikes in vain because his blows are directed against a power greater than himself. He flails nature's irrepressible creative force, and his only tools are death and destruction. Cara de Angel has fulfilled his metaphysical function, he has vanquished death by communicating life; hence, the unconscious exultation in his challenge.[6]

He dies in a dungeon after years of torture and nobody ever knows but that he went to Washington. Little Miguel eventually replaces him in Camila's heart. On the day of his baptism, Pentecost (an ancient Semitic *harvest* festival), as he is reborn in the life of the spirit, life begins to flow back into her for the first time since her husband's disappearance. The rural setting for this occasion is a hymn to maternity, to fecundity, to the harvest of new life, a fitting finale for the novel's motif: "The mocking birds were billing: two ounces of feathers and an infinity of trills. The ewes were busy licking their sucklings ... the colts were romping around the moist-eyed mares. Calves bellowed, their muzzles dripping happiness beside the full udders. Without knowing why, as if life were being reborn in her, she pressed her son against her heart as the christening bells stopped pealing" (pp. 289–90).

IV   *A New Insight*

If we limit our understanding of the novel to the image level, two key questions must go unanswered. What did Miguel do to merit his dreadful punishment? Marry the daughter of an enemy? But even enemies accused of threatening the President's life were punished by a routine death, not by a deliber-

ate mental and physical torture prolonged over years. Did
Miguel's love "redeem" him? If so, in what way? He remains
his master's trained dog to the end. If not redeemed, can the
lengthy exposition of his romance be justified structurally?
It would seem that the author's purpose in leaving these
questions open is to induce the reader to seek answers on
another level.

Cara de Angel's "redemption" is a metaphysical salvation,
not a moral one. He is saved by love which has given him a
new insight. His redemption consists in shifting from a neutral
position in which he let himself be used for destructive ends,
to alignment with the forces of creativity. The change is a
personal one, a matter of inner attitude, but it inevitably
involves the President because unintentionally Miguel begins
to act against him. His purpose in saving Canales, Farfán,
and Camila, is not to injure the President; they are positive
actions, to save lives. But although the President is not aimed
at, he is hit in the recoil because his law is to destroy. Thus
by turning away from the tyrant, Cara de Angel becomes
basically more dangerous to him than if he had merely turned
against him, becoming his personal enemy while remaining
aligned with the same negative camp. Of the two men, the
favorite's comportment is the more serene because his is the
ultimate victory. The President's opposition is marked by
the frenzy of defeat; hence the fantastic punishment he metes
out to his victor, although it is plain that neither man understands nor suspects the nature of their antagonism, which
originates in the necessary polarity of nature.

While the theme of the novel is not intrinsically linked
to the political and social scene, dictatorship is an ideally
chosen setting to provide a ritualistic death or sacrifice such
as tradition ordains for one who, like Miguel, plays the role
of a fertility hero.

CHAPTER 3

Babylonian Mythology in
El Señor Presidente

"Babylon is the symbol of the Terrible Mother." C. G. Jung

FROM fertility as a topic it is only a step to the fertility cults
of mythology, which brings us to another layer of meaning
in *El Señor Presidente*, whereon the idea of procreation and
renewal is further developed. Asturias' preoccupation with
mythology is well known, although it is generally understood
to be confined to Maya mythology. In this case, however,
he also calls upon one of the oldest mythologies of Western
civilization, that of Babylonia, bearing in mind, no doubt,
that the myths of all nations spring from identical psychic
factors.

It should cause no surprise that multiple levels of meaning
are concealed in this work. In the 1920's while it was being
elaborated, Joyce introduced parallel and ambiguous meaning
into his writings to thicken their texture, as well as devices
based on Freud's analytical interpretation of dream work and
its symbolism. Closer to Asturias and probably more appealing,
were examples of similar methods of writing in the literature
of the Maya Indians. Asturias' sympathy and admiration for
Maya culture and its artistic achievements have long been
evident, and he himself has called attention to the growing
influence of indigenous forms of expression on modern Latin
American writers, praising it as a properly American style.
He has pointed out that to the Maya Quiché, who relish word
play and figurative speech, it was normal to use language that
presents different meanings simultaneously; thus, under the
realistic, literal sense of their narratives there lay fanciful and
esoteric significance.[1] There is no reason to assume that Asturias,
having deliberately patterned his work on the indigenous art

and literature of Guatemala would neglect this fascinating aspect of it, all the more since it harmonizes so well with the baroque style and requirements of much Latin American literature.[2]

An accumulation of details indicates that in *El Señor Presidente* Asturias has portrayed in a hidden manner the Babylonian fertility myth of Tammuz and Ishtar, which is the prototype of many subsequent nature cults of the Mediterranean area, for example, Cybele and Attis, Venus and Adonis, Atagartis and Hadad, and the related but more sophisticated Egyptian myth of Isis and Osiris.[3]

It is peculiarly appropriate for Asturias to have juxtaposed Babylon, "the mother of harlots and abominations" (Revelation 17:15), traditionally symbolic of corruption and cruelty, with Guatemala or any other city in the grip of an inhuman dictator. Likewise, the irrational and legitimate terrors experienced by the characters of *El Señor Presidente*, from the idiot Pelele to the President himself, are of the same nature as those known to early man, reflected in many myths and personified in the unreliable Ishtar, the mistress of fate.

Fertility myths attempt to express the mystery of nature's yearly rebirth. The Babylonian myth tells the story of Ishtar, an archetypal Great Mother, the goddess of love, of fertility, and war, mother of mankind and its enemy, who fell in love with Tammuz and whose love proved fatal to him; she is portrayed in part by Camila. The role of Tammuz, who embodies fertility and whose necessary death stands for the coming of winter barrenness, is played by Miguel, although little Miguel, a prolongation of himself born the following spring, represents the resurrected Tammuz and suggests the beginning of a cycle, the agricultural cycle. Unwittingly Camila was the cause of Miguel's death, because it was his interest in her that alienated the President. In some versions of the myth, Ishtar, divested of all possessions, descended into the land of death and fetched back Tammuz. Camila was given up for dead; she brought Miguel to life because the hopelessness of her condition caused him to commit his unconditional acts of love (the warning of Farfán, the nonrational marriage), and as a result he who had been lifeless and barren became alive to the world of love. Like Ishtar, Camila lost all her possessions (family, home) during her bout with death, and the life to which she resuscitated was entirely new. The same thing happened to her again when she brought forth the next Miguel, her son; it was "as if life were being reborn in her" (p. 290). As for Ishtar's notorious faithlessness, it is indicated, not by any act of Camila's, but by the false report to Miguel of her infidelity which was designed to finish him off in his dungeon, and did.

The literal meaning of the word *Babylon* in Assyrian is "gate of God" (*bab-ilu*), and in the novel, "el Portal del Señor" (literally, the gate of the Lord) figures prominently from the first page to the last where, like Babylon, it is being torn down stone by stone. El Portal del Señor was a portico or similar structure adjacent to the Cathedral where the idiot Pelele and other beggars slept, where he throttled the Colonel and to which he was creeping back when he was shot to death by Vásquez. The President ordered the structure torn down to vent his rage over the Colonel's death, and it was over its rubble that the demented dwarf was seen to prance at the novel's end. To one side of el Portal was a neighborhood or street known as the Hundred Doorways (*las Cien Puertas*). Babylon was believed to possess a hundred gates in her famous walls (Herodotus). Where the President mutters drunkenly: "Ni ni mier. . .va," meant to sound like a vulgar expletive, Don Miguel pretends to understand his gibberish to mean Minerva; but if we take away "*mier*" the name Niniva remains (p. 231). Other references to the Near East are liberally scattered through the novel, but we will turn our attention to the similarity between the worship of Ishtar and the story of Camila.

I *Camila as Ishtar*

An important feature of the deity's cult was the annual New Year re-enactment of her union with Tammuz, deemed effective in making fields, barnyards, and nurseries fruitful. The ritual was performed by the current king and a high priestess. In her temple outside the city, Ishtar's priestess prepared for the coming of the King (Tammuz) by taking a ritual bath and singing a love song. Camila's excursion into the country where she took what might now be termed a ritual bath, culminated in the climactic words "they desired each other," which is the burden of the priestess' song. Not until then, after her dip in the pool, had Camila felt anything more than affection toward her husband, a circumstance to which much stress is given, being naturally a matter of anguish for him. This was, as we saw, the key moment of the novel.

The Babylonian hierogamy, or sacred marriage, was consummated in a chamber located in the highest part of the temple; it symbolized the union of heaven and earth, wherein the sky god of thunder and rain descended upon the earth goddess to fecundate her. This is portrayed by Camila and Miguel's last hours together, when they lay in the upper room and when, presumably, little Miguel was conceived. A heavy storm preceded their embrace, rain had blown into their bedroom. Now the storm is over and in the yard outside, a chicken dies at the hands of the cook. By presenting parallel accounts of these two actions, it was seen that Asturias suggests the continuity of life in nature and the analogy between the ending of life and the beginning.[4] The fruitful promise of the gods' nuptials is rendered in the novel by the account of little Miguel's baptism (the Christian death and rebirth ritual) on the feast of Pentecost, where the domestic animals share with Camila in the exuberance of new life. As she stands there happily surrounded by birds and beasts, she brings to mind the nature goddesses entitled "Lady of the Beasts," frequently represented in ancient statuary.[5] At Babylon, part of the New Year festivities following the sacred nuptials consisted in a ceremonial banquet for the elite, attended by musicians, priests, and singer-poets. This corresponds to the soirée given by the President to which Camila and Miguel were invited. On the way to the palace Camila was frightened by the speed of the carriage. "Isht. . . . quiet!" murmurs Cara de Angel to comfort her. He means sh-sh, but the unusual way of spelling it suggests the name Ishtar. Entering the reception hall the couple passed near a poet who was declaiming to a group of guests: "At the moment they were passing by, this man was

raising his arm with a slow gesture and opening his hand as
if instead of speaking he were about to release a pigeon"
(p. 254). This hand, uplifted in Camila's direction, makes the
gesture of obeisance called "hand-raising to Ishtar," which
accompanied prayers to that deity. Pigeons are fertility symbols
sacred to the *Magna Mater* (Great Mother). Camila herself
is described here in a way that evokes one of the countless
primitive female figurines stressing fecundity; all eyes were
upon her because of "her exotic beauty, her green eyes, clear
and soulless, her slender body, copied in the white silk of her
dress, her firm, full breasts" (p. 255). The cold, expressionless
eyes, chiseled in emerald perhaps, are those of an idol; the
shiny white dress which moulds her body indicates that the
statue is a nude of alabaster or ivory, which is confirmed when
someone whispers that she is not wearing a corset. Later in
the book Camila's figure is compared to a guitar, which is the
precise aspect of some primitive figurines used in fertility
rites.[6] Accentuation of hips and breast characterizes the Great
Mother as dispenser of life and nourishment.

Corresponding to the musicians, priests, and poets of the
Babylonian feast, a native marimba enlivens the President's
fiesta and as Camila is introduced to His Excellency, a literary
priest celebrates her beauty by quoting some appropriate
verses. More poetry follows as the dictator commands the poet
to recite something good like the Song of Songs. The significance of repeatedly linking the Song of Solomon with the young
couple lies in the fact that this biblical hymn of love was
originally derived from a fertility ritual in honor of Tammuz.[7]
At this juncture the President is seen suddenly padding off
through the curtains like a jaguar to his guests' terrified
amazement. While on the Maya folklore level the incident
indicates that this animal is the President's *nahual*, that is to
say his animal-protector, whose shape he can assume at will,
it also corroborates the Babylonian interpretation: Mesopo-
tamians were susceptible to a similar experience, namely
lycanthropy, whereby a man imagines himself to be a wild
animal. According to traditional exegesis, King Nebuchadnezzar
of Babylon was so afflicted (Daniel 4:30, 5:21).

In the vague accounts of Semitic deities, Ishtar is the

daughter of a water-god and the sister of Shamash, the sun-
god. These two gods seem to be combined in the person of
General Canales, Camila's father. His name has a water
connotation and calls to mind that canals were vital to Babylon.
Great numbers of them, large and small, interlaced that arid
region, a fact which·is illustrated in the novel by the large
family of the General: the Canales, cousins, uncles and aunts
swarmed like insects, complained Camila.

On the other hand, her father has a nickname, Chamarrita,
that is reminiscent of Shamash, the sun god of justice; his
fury at the injustices he discovered during his flight through
the mountains supports his interest in justice. Riding out
of Las Aldeas (Caldea?) he shoots down an extortioner. His
manner of dispensing justice may seem arbitrary for a mere
mortal, but it is proper for a god; the first Indian to follow
Canales had immediately sensed this quality of unearthliness
in him; he looked upon the General as a fetish, or some kind
of god.

On warm afternoons when Camila was a child, her father
would sit on the balcony, nodding to passing acquaintances,
while she, alone and bored, peeped out from behind the curtains
in the front room. Her father could be seen through the bars
of the balcony wearing a white linen shirt, his elbows resting
on a satin pillow. One of the friends who stopped to talk with
him, sallow-faced and hook-nosed (the Semitic features of
a Babylonian), carried a gold-knobbed walking stick which he
kept raising to his nose as he talked, "as if to smell the gold"
(p. 83). The scene is like one of the Assyrian bas-reliefs depicting Shamash in his shrine receiving worship; flattening
one's nose with a rod was a ritual gesture of abasement peculiar
to the cult of Shamash; gold was, moreover, his symbol as sun
god. Linen was a quality fabric used for sacred garments.[8]
Camila watching from behind the curtain is like one of the
temple statues of Ishtar that stood in a niche, generally concealed by a veil to protect it from profane eyes.

When Camila was thought to be dying a priest came to ad-
minister the sacrament of penance. Her girlish faults stand
out in contrast with the evil that weighs over the city. Indeed,
one of the things she mentions in confession is no fault at

all: she rode a horse, sitting like a man, in the presence of some Indians. The priest rebukes her for trying to equal man when God made her a woman, and he warns her to stop imitating the devil who fell because he wanted to be God. What would prompt such a farfetched analogy? In terms of the goddess Ishtar the explanation is simple: Camila's posture recalls the Great Mother's ritual exhibitionism, a sign of her fertility, as seen in primitive seals and figurines. The Indians who were with Camila represent the primitive peoples who would understand such symbolism. Fertility was equally essential for the goddess's male counterpart, as manifested in phallic rituals. The parallel situation whereby Asturias draws attention to the procreative organs of Miguel-Tammuz occurs at a café where he joins his friends hurriedly buttoning his fly, a detail for which no other explanation offers itself. As for the priest's admonition not to ape the devil who wanted to be God, it is amusingly apt for Camila in her role of Ishtar, recalling that to the early Christians and to the Jews, Ishtar, like all pagan gods, was just a manifestation of the Evil One by which he sought to receive for himself the worship that was due to God.

When Ishtar was venerated as a corn goddess, she was accompanied by a serpent that was considered to be identical with herself; serpents are universal emblems of regeneration and renewal, and in the novel Ishtar's ophidian companion is portrayed by La Masacuata, the tavern keeper who nursed Camila through her illness; *masacuata*, her sobriquet, is the name for a harmless Guatemalan snake.

II   *Don Miguel as Tammuz*

Don Miguel makes his first appearance in the novel near the garbage pit where the woodsman saw him. The chapter is entitled "Cara de Angel" ("Angel's Face"), but we do not know at this point that it is a man's name. Throughout the scene he retains an aura of supernatural mystery because we see him through the eyes of the peasant for whom he had the markings of an angel. Don Miguel had suddenly emerged from a clump of pine trees. In spite of his piercing black eyes, there was a womanish look about him: blond hair, delicate mouth, skin like golden marble (another statue?); his hat resembled a dove. Evergreens, especially pines, and the prolific dove, are associated with fertility gods, who generally have a feminine appearance; for example, Bacchus and Adonis. Tammuz, congeneric with Adonis, was a youth whose marvelous beauty won the favor of Ishtar; in the liturgy bewailing his death, he is called bright-eyed, and in works of art he is sometimes shown with the oversized black eyes that characterize the Mesopotamian style. Not only to the woodsman, but to an old lady whom he helped a few days later Don Miguel was like an angel, yet those black eyes were satanic, and even Camila felt their "diabolic phosphorescences" (p. 132). Indeed, an ominous description of him runs through the novel: "He was as handsome and evil as Satan" (p. 39). Good angel or bad—or both—Miguel Cara de Angel (literally, Michael Angel's Face) has the mark of a supernatural being. His name is doubly angelic since Michael is traditionally the leader of the angels; besides, in Hebrew Michael means "who is like God." It is a name that would also befit Tammuz, the mortal who, due to the *angelic beauty of his countenance* that captivated Ishtar, became immortal, *like a god*, when she fetched him back from the dead. However, there was one Semitic people for whom Miguel-Tammuz by his very nature could only be evil—the Jews. The worship of Tammuz was one of the abominations which Yahveh showed to Ezekiel (8:14). From this point of view the strange refrain, "He was as handsome and evil as Satan" is clear: Tammuz was beautiful to behold, as is the fertile vegetation he represents, but to deify him, to worship the reproductive forces of nature as if they operated independently of God, was as abhorrent as the Adversary. (Naturism or adoration of the powers of nature was an ever-present temptation for the Israelites, exposed as they were to the example of their pagan neighbors.)

Among the legends concerning Tammuz' death, one tells that he was torn to pieces by demons, another that he was drowned. Both fates are intimated of Miguel: when he was beaten in the freight car by Farfán, pieces of his flesh and tufts of his hair were torn off his face and scalp. Later, one of the rumors that circulated concerning his disappearance was that he had died at sea.

III   *The President as the Great Mother*

In order to portray the ambivalent nature of Ishtar, that is to say, the beneficent and the malefic aspects of the earth, Asturias resorts to another character, as he used the two Miguels for Tammuz. Thus, while the loveliness of the Great Mother is personified by Camila, her fearful aspect is portrayed by the President, for just as Ishtar favored then destroyed Tammuz, the tyrant favored and then arbitrarily destroyed Miguel.

The archetype of the Terrible Mother is rooted in man's primordial experience which is that the same life-giving earth becomes the devourer of his body in death. The womb of the Great Mother was not only the beginning of man, it was also his end. In one of his masterly metaphors, Asturias has dramatized this idea by identifying the living death that Miguel suffered after his arrest with the notion of being buried in the womb of the earth. But if the President is the Terrible Mother, then the underground prison wherein his victims waste away, and which is an extention of himself, may be considered the Terrible Mother's womb. That this was Asturias' intention seems apparent.

In the novel, little Miguel is still in Camila's womb when we first hear of him; once, while waiting for an audience with the President, she felt the infant kick her as if to say, "Let's get away from here!" (p. 286). Don Miguel ends up in a similar situation, for the tiny cell in which he has been left to rot has the markings of a living tomb or womb. For him, the President's dungeon is verily the Great Mother's womb. Moisture oozes through the sides of the cavernous vault like rainwater into a grave. After long dry spells, Miguel licked the dampness to satisfy his thirst, although it was like "blood from a crushed scorpion" (p. 292. Scorpions often symbolized the death-underworld aspect of Ishtar).[9] Mention of the moisture being blood, which he consumes, suggests that the walls are a living tissue, so that simultaneously with the

connotation of a burial vault, the damp walls bring to mind
the maternal membrane enclosing an embryo, thus illustrating
the ambivalent nature of the archetypal womb. The puddle
which often covers the floor of Miguel's tiny cell forces him
to squat on a stone in a fetal position. The bucket in which
he satisfies his needs and the one containing his soup are
lowered into his cell by a cord, which must be the umbilical
cord. He pounds on the walls and kicks on the floor of his
"womb," just as his son does in Camila's. These walls, however,
are described as "intestinal vaults," suggesting a caecum.
Rather than a womb, for Don Miguel it is a maw, a stinking
bowel that dismembers him and reduces him to putrefaction;
indeed he dies of putrid dysentery, a suitable fate for the
victim of an agricultural rite, destined to fertilize the soil.
It was also appropriate that when Farfán beat him, he should
fall in the *manure* on the floor of the boxcar.

IV   *Fedina as the Great Mother*

Another version of the same process wherein the earth
reabsorbs the product of its own matrix is found in the chapter
entitled "The Living Tomb," where Fedina Rodas, unbalanced
by the torture of her son, begins to imagine that his shriveled
corpse, now more like a fetus than a baby, has become part of
her own body again. It occurs to her that she herself shall
be his tomb. To this effect she closes her eyes and crouches
in a corner of her cell, dark, motionless, and silent in imitation
of a sepulcher, and crushes the tiny body against her own.
"The idea of being the tomb of her son caressed her heart
like a balm. Hers was the happiness of the women who buried
themselves with their lovers in the sacred Orient. And in
greater measure, because she was not burying herself with
her son; she was his living tomb, his last earthly cradle" (p. 155).
Notably fitting is the reference here to the Royal Tombs of
Ur in ancient Sumeria.[10] The Rodas child is another figure
of Miguel-Tammuz, buried in the living tomb, the bosom of
his mother, the Earth. Here Fedina is the Great Mother in
her negative aspect and another surrogate of Camila (through

the baby's baptism, which Camila was sponsoring, they were to have been *comadres*, literally, co-mothers of the child).

To confirm Fedina's identity as a Great Mother, there is an earlier scene where, alone in the cell, she says her evening prayers. She recites the *Memorare*, prayer to the Virgin as Mother of *Mercy*, imploring protection; then she sinks to the ground with her arms extended, and her arms seem to grow very long until they embrace all the other prisoners like herself, all those who suffer injustice, all those at the point of death (these are invocations taken from another part of Evening Prayers). Does she not evoke one of those madonnas of *Mercy* pictured with her mantle stretched over a crowd of petitioners? The mantle and attitude symbolize the Christian Great Mother's protective concern for mankind, the attribute which is repeatedly invoked in the *Memorare*, given in full in the text for greater emphasis. In a yet earlier scene, when she was still home, we saw Fedina standing dramatically with her son at her breast, momentarily immobilized like a stone effigy by her husband who was prostrate before her, hugging her feet, a prey to foreboding hallucinations.

V *Additional Mythological Parallels*

In most of the Great Mother myths, as in Ishtar's, she loves a beautiful youth, causes his death, weeps over him and bewails his loss, then brings him back to life. The ritual commemorating these events was enacted by women devotees who imitated her sorrow, filling the air with loud wailing, their hair streaming, and their breast bared. All this is portrayed at the brothel, where Fedina is taken a day or so after the baby's death. The presence of the infant is detected by its smell; it has become wizened and dry like a seed—for that is what a fertility god is, a seed, the origin of himself. With gusto the prostitutes organize a wake. In a bedroom reeking, appropriately, of "old sperm," the infant is laid out, and a great, big crying session begins: for each woman it is her own son who has died. As the orgy progresses, one of the drunken girls, bathed in tears with her breast uncovered, intones a lullaby. These weeping prostitutes are the famous women worshipers mourning for Tammuz as the ritual demanded (Ezekiel 8:14). It was, incidentally, the obligation of Ishtar's devotees to practice ritual prostitution.

Camila did her own mourning over Miguel, of course, during her long months of pregnancy; then, like Ishtar, she brought him back to life—in her son.

Fertility gods such as Tammuz were like drones serving the queen bee (Miguel was actually called a drone in the sense of idler, by General Canales), and since their only purpose was to arouse the desire of the goddess by their beauty, they were killed off as soon as their function was accomplished. They were the vegetation itself which is harvested as soon as it produces new seed for the next crop. This is a second reason why so much stress is laid on whether or not Camila desires Miguel, and why the moment in which she does is the climax of the novel.[11] As in the myth, Miguel is cut down as soon as the child is conceived.

The relationship of the Great Goddess to her son-lovers was one of complete dominance; this is depicted by Cara de Angel's absorption in his wife. It was so obvious that his enemies mocked him with the joke that since his marriage to the Canales girl, his name should be changed to "Miguel Canales." The goddess' undifferentiated love for each son-lover is expressed in Camila's transition dream where she saw a ball bounce away from her and disappear (her husband) while the candy in her mouth (her son) grew until it filled her whole being. The same transition is expressed again in the finale as little Miguel becomes the focus of her new life the following spring.

One of the Ishtar legends tells that she managed to return from the nether world with the help of two sexless creatures sent to her rescue—sexless, because being neither man nor woman they were exempt from the law of the underworld. In *El Señor Presidente* the sexless beings are represented by the effeminate Tícher, who rescued Camila from death by telling Miguel to marry her. Tícher is also Tyche, the goddess of Fate, one of Ishtar's most important titles. On the occasion

of the Babylonian New Year, Ishtar was enjoined to fix the
king's destiny. True to his name, Tícher fixed Miguel's destiny
when he counseled marriage, because marriage to Camila
led to the favorite's death. When after the marriage Tícher
quoted Shakespeare to Miguel saying: "Make thee another
self for love of *me*," he was Ishtar speaking to Tammuz, urging
him to be sure and reproduce himself to supply her with her
next year's son-lover!

Without dwelling upon the sanguinary temperament, and
other unpleasant characteristics shared by the tyrant and
Ishtar, we should note that her essential function as mistress
of fate is duly ascribed to the President: complaining to his
favorite of having to do everything himself for a nation of
inert citizens, he describes himself as acting the part of the
blind goddess Fortuna (the Roman equivalent of Tyche)
through the national lottery which he operates. Repeatedly
throughout the book mention is made of chance, destiny,
blind forces, and inevitability, reflecting the fatalistic state
of mind of a people whose life and fortune depend on the whims
of a bloodthirsty dictator; fatalism also characterized the
attitudes of Semitic peoples; it was in Babylonia and Chaldea
that blind chance was first deified, and it was there that astrolo-
gy originated.[12]

One begins to see that many of the characters in *El Señor
Presidente* are homologues of either Camila or Miguel, or to
put it differently, they portray further aspects of Ishtar and
Tammuz. The tavern keeper, La Masacuata, and her sweetheart, Lucio Vásquez, the policeman with the effeminate
voice, as a couple, are foils to the protagonist couple on two
levels. Their byplay in the shabby little bar, where they roll
on the floor, entwined like a pair of snakes, augurs Miguel's
intended conduct with Camila later that night in the same
setting, and the contrast of Miguel's actual behavior sets off
the tremendous change that Camila had already effected in
him. Like Miguel, Vásquez is put to death by the President
shortly after intercourse with his partner. Ishtar and Tammuz
are, mythologically speaking, a pair of snakes as can be seen
on early Babylonian seals representing their union, and these

symbolic, life-giving reptiles are the origin of the entwined
serpents of the caduceus which the medical profession aptly
chose as its emblem.

VI   *The Tammuz Myth in Depth Psychology*

Significantly, the men in the novel are generally dominated
by their womenfolk, or at least their wife, mother or sweetheart has the stronger personality, which is the case with the
mythological pair.[13] In fact, the Great Mother finally overpowers most of the male characters, which is to say that they
return to the womb and are consequently functional replicas
of Miguel. In order fully to understand this, it is necessary
to review the significance of the archetype in this connection.

The analytical psychology of C. G. Jung, according to
which all myths have psychic relevance, understands fertility
myths involving the Great Goddess and her phallic consorts
to be symptomatic of that stage in the growth of human consciousness when the adolescent ego is engaged in struggling
toward self-consciousness and independence against the negative pull of the unconscious, *but cannot hold out*; the struggle
inevitably ends in flight and surrender. The individual ego
can only pass beyond this stage by adopting an aggressive and
heroic attitude toward the unconscious (personified as the
Great Mother). Thus the fertility myth is followed by the
myth of the *hero*, such as Perseus slaying the Gorgon or Theseus, the Minotaur. True to his role, Miguel reached but did
not pass this stage; he fled from the Great Mother-President
and was overcome, regressing to the original state of unconsciousness which is designated by Jung as the Great Round
or the Uroboros. Among the earliest symbols of the Great
Mother are the circle and the sphere, the latter as container
or womb, and the circle as a duplicate of the snake eating its
tail. This serpent or dragon feeding on itself is a figurative
expression of perfect self-sufficiency and of the dawn state of
undifferentiation, before the ego begins to develop, before
pain and want; it is the state experienced by the individual
at birth and known to Jungians as the Uroboros.[14] Now for a

look at the men in the novel who regress to the Great Mother, noting the emphasis given to motherhood and circles.

The wife of the dwarf Benjamín was a barrel—a mountain of flesh; she could pick him up and hold him like a child. On one such occasion he mutters: "A wet nurse, not a wife, that's what the priest gave me the day he married us!" (p. 57). By the end of the novel he has lost his mind; that is, he has regressed to the unconscious (Great Mother).

After the student is released from prison he returns to his mother's. As he enters the door she is leading a recitation of the rosary, an endless *circle* of beads.

Pelele, the idiot, dreams happily of his mother and of the Virgin (the Good Mother) while lying on a rubbish heap in a *circle* of vultures intent on devouring him (the Terrible Mother). He prefigures Miguel dreaming of Camila and *his* mother, while disintegrating in the prison-tomb of the President. He is a psychological replica of Miguel.

La Marrana (the Sow), nickname of Farfán's favorite prostitute, intoxicated him by her "serpentine" wiles while betraying him to the President; she illustrates the Circe aspect of the Great Mother that drives men insane and transforms them into swine; such drunken orgies as Farfán's are an essential part of Tammuz and Dionysus cults, and from the viewpoint of psychology they stand for the dissolution of the ego and return to the womb.

The sacristan was in prison for years because by mistake he tore down a poster in the church vestibule about the President's *mother* instead of one about Our Lady of O; this little known feast is celebrated December 18 in honor of the Virgin's *motherhood*, drawing its name from the "O" antiphons sung the week before Christmas (this circle, "O", is a sneaky one!) When released he was ordered to wear his cassock in the street (unlawful in Guatemala) which in this context is interpreted as "women's" clothes, therefore a sign that he remains under feminine domination.

The male pianist at the brothel used makeup and was nicknamed Violeta; he duplicates the priests of Cybele (Galli) who mutilated themselves and wore women's garments.

In his underground prison Miguel was not definitively beaten until he heard and *believed* the false report that his wife had become the President's mistress. Then, when he was no longer able to distinguish between the Good Mother and the Terrible, and Camila became identified with the President, but not until then, he reverted to the embrace of the unconscious. At the moment he heard this news, says the text, the delicate sound of a reptile was heard in the dark. There follows a play on words; Spanish *comer* means both to eat and to itch: "From then on, the prisoner began to scratch himself, as if his body, which he no longer felt, was itching," or, as if *his body was eating him.*[15] Awareness of pain is the beginning of consciousness, whereas Miguel no longer felt his body; furthermore, his body was "eating him," thereby giving form to the self-consuming reptile, symbolic of the Uroborus to which he was reverting.

This passage, although taken from a police report to the President, cannot be read literally even on the image level; the language is poetic and figurative, as in so much of the novel. For instance, there was no reptile in Miguel's cell, and the "delicate sound" was made by the shattering of his hope, or at most it came from the agony in his breath, which would have the same significance. When Asturias thus avails himself of ambiguity to extend his fiction to the field of psychology, his device is in perfect harmony with his usual poetic prose style as well as with the very psychic processes in which he is interested. Poetry with its unexplained symbols; Maya literature with its puns and parallel meanings favored by Asturias; and the unconscious as it manifests itself through dreams, fantasies, myths: each and all of these modes of communication require searching interpretation to be understood.

It seems clear that Asturias' intention is to carry his myth through to its psychic implications and to apply these not only to the protagonist Cara de Angel but to the latter's various alter egos throughout the book and, consequently, to the male segment of society at large.

VII   *The Archetype of Dictatorship*

We are not to conclude, however, that to Asturias the

culture of a people who tolerates a regime such as the President's has not developed beyond the stage of psychic adolescence. The reality of the situation is more in the nature of a regression. Indeed, Asturias views the phenomenon of Latin American despotism as an awakening of primitive instincts and presidents such as his as modern incarnations of preternatural forces that touch off an archaic response of terror and worship. He discusses this concept in a lecture entitled *"El Señor Presidente* as Myth". Recalling that in modern life the novel holds the place formerly held by the recital of myths in primitive societies, he explains that *El Señor Presidente* should be counted among what might be called mythological narratives. Underneath its literary and political elements, there can be found, in the shape of a Latin American president, a concept of ancestral and fabulous power that belongs to our times in appearance only. The dictator is the myth-man, the superior being (because, like it or not, that is what he is) who fulfills the functions of tribal chief among primitive people, anointed by sacral potencies. He keeps himself invisible, like God, for the less corporeal he remains, the more mythical he will be deemed to be. The fascination he exerts even over his enemies, the supernatural aura that surrounds him, everything about him concurs in actualizing that which is mythical and outside chronological time.

Could the final essence of *El Señor Presidente* be that it is really a myth, the survival of a great initial myth whose weight still maintains its semireligious dominion over certain countries, with its fanatical followers and its reprobates imprisoned in indescribable hells? Do not such presidents attain the stature of supernatural beings? Are they not awful, terrifying realities yet at the same time something like religious punishments and, as such, beings outside of reality? Around these presidents, a sort of ritual develops, implied by the so-called personality cult, although in truth it is not directed to the current personality but to the ancestral force it represents. . . . In one of the last chapters we assist at the Dance of Tohil, the Maya Quiché divinity who demanded human sacrifice. What else but sacrifices did the President exact? Those were not executions but human sacrifices. . . .[16]

To depth psychologists of the Jungian school the ancestral force that Asturias is talking about is in reality a psychic force dwelling in the unconscious mind, which, when active, is projected outside the affected individual and perceived as an objective reality. Primitive man personified the images through which he perceived his psychic energies as gods and described them in myths. These archaic images or archetypes of the collective unconscious which all men share are like a dry riverbed, says Jung; the deeper the channel, the longer the river once flowed there, and the more likely is the water to return. He wrote this in 1936 in connection with the rise of Hitlerism, which he saw as the reawakening of Wotan, the ancient Germanic war god who stirred up the frenzy of the Berserkers. According to Jung, the Wotan archetype came to life again and took possession of the German people.[17] Likewise, the dictatorship that *El Señor Presidente* depicts can be understood as the reactivation in a people of an archaic experience and pattern of behavior, once personified, as Asturias indicates, in the Maya Quiché god, Tohil. No longer consciously acceptable as a god, the Tohil archetype when experienced is now projected on the dictator; the despot becomes a supernatural figure in the unconscious estimation of his subjects, to be served in a ritual and propitiated by blood offerings. The nature and attributes of a man who can be so defined are residues of ancestral experience projected upon him by the eye of the beholder. The projection he bears is an archetype which we recognize as stemming from the Terrible Mother, for no matter how strongly overlaid it may be with patriarchal elements, the symbolism of blood sacrifice belongs to the feminine. The act of tearing out palpitating human hearts, which Tohil, like the Aztec gods, required, corresponds to the husking of corn, and is essentially a rite of fertility and renewal connected with the Great Earth Mother.[18] While an archetype like Tohil is shaped by the ethos and characteristics peculiar to a nation or tribe, its basic pattern belongs to the universal experience of man, Babylonian, Maya, Germanic, whatever.

Aside from the psychological accuracy of Asturias' diagnosis, he has known how to exploit it in a highly effective manner. Depicted as a modern instance of the Tohil myth, the Guatemalan dictator is linked with national prehistory on one plane, while on another he embodies the corresponding archetypal image of Ishtar from one of the oldest Western mythologies, thus rendering in universal, cyclic, and psychological dimensions a typically Central American syndrome, without in anyway minimizing its local relevancy.

Another major accomplishment of the novel is the closeness of its structure and its verbal economy despite the broad range of society caught up in the conflict. It is a dramatic novel shaped by action that moves forward swiftly, logically, and purposefully, achieving, notably by the dynamic use of foreshadowing, a tightly knit design.

The mythical framework is not what gives the work its form, for it has its own self–sustaining structure. But the myth does provide further meaning to it. It directs our vision from the absorbing passions of its present-day setting to the continuity of history, highlighting the immutability of the human psyche and our bond with the men of antiquity. The myth begins and ends precisely where Miguel's story begins and ends. All we are told of his past is that he had a mother and that she had a white rose in her window . . . which is a symbol of the Good Mother. His immediate past was bound up with the President, the other aspect of the Mother. This is precisely all we need to know of a fertility god: his relationship with his mother-wife is his only reason for being. Camila, on the other hand, has a past from before the novel began: her childhood, her cousins, her vacations and her games. She has a future extending beyond the limits of the book. Likewise, the myth of Tammuz and Ishtar is Tammuz' story (or Adonis'), not Ishtar's (or Venus') for many other adventures and legends were attached to her, whereas this is Tammuz' one and only: his whole life is contained in it. As for the recurring duplication of the figures of Miguel and Camila in the novel's other characters, these are a means of suggesting the annually recurring cycle of their myth. The unity and integral organization of *El Señor Presidente* are eminent technical achievements.

A final word on the epigraph of this chapter. In his great book, *Symbols of Transformation*, which has had so important an influence on literature, Jung indicates that a substitute symbol for the Great Mother is the city, as being a great enclosure or container. City symbolism is particularly developed in St. John's Apocalypse, where the heavenly Jerusalem obviously represents the positive aspect of the Great Mother and where "Babylon is the symbol of the Terrible Mother."[19] All of this brings us back to the aptness of the analogy Asturias draws between the city of the novel and Babylon because, insofar as the subjects of the President accept his dictatorship, they succumb to the Terrible Mother—they regress to the unconscious.

CHAPTER 4

Hombres de maíz

HOMBRES DE MAÍZ (Corn Men, 1949) is among the least understood of Asturias' major novels. Some critics have disregarded it altogether; others have sensed the breadth of the author's vision but judged that it was not successfully carried out. In a recent book, Luis Harss has stated that it is probably for this novel that Asturias will be remembered. Nevertheless, he goes on to say that Asturias is not a thinker and that his novels are conceptually weak. On the other hand, the Peruvian critic Luis Alberto Sánchez reports that during the 1920's, in Paris, Asturias was an assiduous student of Orientalism, mythology, and anthropology with a strong side interest in occultism, and that he was considered very learned. It would appear that his Paris reputation was well deserved, for whatever modest disclaimers he may make, the evidence of *Hombres de maíz* alone shows him to be a profound and erudite thinker. It is a novel so rich and so full as to appear confusing. Its surface difficulties and bulky complexity lend the book a certain elusiveness that tantalizes. This may have put some readers off, causing them to complain that it lacks unity and to wonder if the author was sure of what he was doing.[1]

Asturias knew very well what he was doing, of course, having produced a calculated work of art. He has intricately structured his novel on a firm basis of analytical psychology, and at this level the unity and consistency of the work is apparent; the mystery, the magic, the legends all find their reason for being, their justification, without being explained away or losing any of their charm and beauty. *Hombres de maíz* dramatizes the quest for the feminine principle which is every man's quest for completion. In order to reach this meaning, however, it is necessary to analyze attentively and to piece together many scattered items, some of which may seem insignificant. The task is fascinating, instructive, and time consuming, for as Asturias himself admits, no concessions have been made to the reader. It is a task not unlike that which faces the psychologist when presented with a patient's dreams; he must study them minutely, draw on many fields of knowledge and human experience, ponder and grope until he begins to perceive their hidden messages. Even so he may have barely scratched the surface of the full meaning, as may be the case here with *Hombres de maíz*. Regardless, the effort is necessary if the reader is to obtain some concept of the scope of Asturias' vision before venturing to evaluate his writings. The following a-nalysis is an outline of the material the novelist presents and a method by which better to understand it.

The title of *Hombres de maíz* refers to the Maya Indians' belief that their flesh was made of corn. The Creator and Maker gods had first tried clay, then wood, but neither was satisfactory. Finally, corn meal was found to be the ideal substance.[2] Although Asturias divides the novel into six parts and nineteen chapters of widely varying lengths, its subject matter falls naturally into three sections. At first reading the three sections appear to be so divergent and unrelated, each with its own characters and topic, as to credit the charge that the book lacks unity; some of the characters from each section meet toward the end but this is not sufficient to consolidate the three plots. The novel's unity rests, rather, upon the fact that the first two sections describe events that, by taking on the weightiness of legends, become moving factors in the third section.

The first section tells the epic of the Indians' fight to preserve their sense of identity against those who would change their ways, disregard their beliefs and, in the name of progress, force an unacceptable way of life upon them. Specifically, they will not tolerate that corn, which is to them a sacred sustenance, be grown for commercial purposes in their mountains. A detachment of soldiers is sent to the rescue of the *maiceros* (corn growers) to protect them from the Indian sharpshooters, but it is unable to subdue the guerrillas because they are led by the Invincible Gaspar Ilóm. The officer in charge of the

government troops, Colonel Godoy, eventually gets the better
of him, but only through ruse: he induces friends of Gaspar to
poison him during a fiesta, and when the cacique is disposed
of, his followers are quickly dispatched. As a result of this
calamity, a curse is said to be laid by the spirits of dead ancestors
and sorcerers upon all those who were involved in the war
against Gaspar.

Accordingly, within the space of seven years each poisoner
along with his entire family meets a violent death. Machojón
and his wife, the false friends who applied the poison to the
cacique, died in a huge fire, and young Machojón, their son,
disappeared mysteriously; it was said that he was carried
away in a cloud of fireflies and condemned to wander forever
in the skies. The pharmacist Zacatón who sold the poison,
and the seven members of his family, had their heads chopped
off while sleeping by the Tecún brothers who were fulfilling a
spell cast by a witch doctor, Curandero Seven-year Stag.
Colonel Godoy, from whom the idea originated, found himself
trapped in a mountain cirque also by the Tecún brothers, and
burned to death with some of his men. Finally, a general curse
of sterility was laid on the remaining soldiers.

The second section is entitled "María Tecún" after a woman
who never appears in it at all, the runaway wife of a blind
beggar. She left him taking their numerous children and every
movable object they owned including part of the roof. At
first Goyo Yic, the blind man, tried to follow her through the
mountains calling her and his children, filling the canyons
and ravines with his cries: "María Tecúúúú ÚÚÚn! María Tecúúúú ÚÚÚn!"[3] This takes place a generation after the events of
the first section because María Tecún was a baby in the Zacatón
household who was overlooked when the family was decapitated
by the Tecún brothers. Goyo had found her crying under
her mother's bed. He took her home, brought her up, and gave
her that name; eventually he married her. The fifty pages of
this section deal with his search for her. He scraped up enough
money to have the cataracts removed from his eyes and began
to peddle women's trinkets. For years he traveled through
mountain villages attending fiestas in the hope of recognizing
María Tecún among his customers by the sound of her voice.

Once he found a wounded opossum (tacuazín) and kept it as a mascot. The name he gave his pet eventually became his own nickname, Tatacuazín (*tata* means papa); but like María, the opossum ran away from him. Found drunk in the outskirts of a village, he was erroneously accused of contraband and sentenced to a three-year term in an island fortress off the Atlantic coast. His story is picked up again in the last pages of the novel where his eldest son, also unjustly condemned to prison, arrives on the island; later Goyo meets María Tecún herself when she comes to visit her son.

This entire episode is presented in a realistic style. In the third section we see the facts of Goyo's drama distorted and transformed into a legendary tale. It frequently happens for popular memory to change facts to make them fit a deeper, more satisfying truth. In contrast with this section, the essentials of the first section have already been distorted by legend, and it is up to the reader to discover their meaning; hence, the need for interpretation.

The third section is as long as the other two combined and it is the core of the novel. It centers around Nicho Aquino who personally knows none of the characters mentioned so far. He is an Indian mail carrier who connects a mountain village, San Miguel de Acatán, with the capital, a two-day trip on foot. On the day the story begins he comes home to find that his young wife has mysteriously disappeared. The next morning, as there is still no sign of her, he goes to the tavern of Aleja Cuevas and gets drunk; he has with him a bright red shawl which was to have been a present for his wife. Aleja, the tavern keeper, takes a fancy to the shawl and tries to talk him into giving it to her; later when drink gets the better of him, she wants to filch it, but Nicho has wound it around his arm and even in his stupor he does not let go of it.

Three weeks later, having spent time in jail for his drunkenness, he leaves for what will be his last mail trip, carrying two sacks of mail. Jazmín, his little white dog with black forepaws, goes with him. He stops overnight at Moncha's place in the hamlet of Tres Aguas, but being unable to sleep he goes out to the patio and starts telling Jazmín about why he misses his wife. An old man comes out to join him, coughing and shuffling, and proffering a stream of advice about insomnia and the dangers of talking to oneself. He is a pleasant, wrinkled fellow with white hair and hands that are blackened as if he had dipped them in dye. Giving advice is the favorite pastime of old men, he chuckles, though they themselves never did what they tell others to do.

When Nicho resumes his trip the old man sets out with him, and as they walk along the letter carrier confides his troubles to his new friend. After listening sympathetically and questioning him, the man says mysteriously: "Come with me, I know where your wife is" (p. 176). Nicho's eyes fill with grateful tears; these are the words he has been waiting to hear ever since the night he came home' and found the house empty. He follows the man with black hands off the highway (*camino real*, which literally can be translated, road of reality), through fields of yellow flowers, and suddenly all three of them fall into a ravine in a shower of stones. When he pulls himself together, Nicho sees the old man making signs for him to go into a nearby cave before disappearing in the dust and taking Jazmín with him. Nicho obeys and, still carrying his two sacks of mail, he follows a passageway into the mountain until he comes to a beautiful, high grotto and a lake. There he meets another old man who also has black hands like the first one. This man tells Nicho that he is the Curandero Seven-year Stag, one of the sorcerers who laid the curse on Gaspar's, enemies, and a descendant of the great mountain spirits, Those Who Strike Flints Together, of Maya Cakchiquel lore. (The Curandero was a real man in the first section of the novel.)

Through him Nicho learns what happened to his wife Isaura. She had not run away at all. She had fallen into an abandoned well while walking through a field. The sole witness to her demise was her little dog Jazmín who was still whimpering when the master came back to his empty house. After Nicho recovers from his grief, he proceeds deep into the mountain with the Curandero as his guide. They witness wondrous scenes and see many people: the dead, such as the Invincible Gaspar Ilóm, and those yet to be born. This underground world is the alpha and omega of all things for the Maya Indians,

the nadir from which they, like the sun, have their origin
and to which they return after death. This explains why
Nicho passed through the field of yellow flowers on his way
to the cave, for the Maya associate them with the dead (there
was also a field of yellow flowers in Hades).

Another essential aspect of Maya culture is the belief in
nahualism; that is, the ability a man has to assume the shape
of his guardian animal. The Curandero's *nahual* or bush soul
was, of course, a stag; Nicho's *nahual* is a coyote, and he assumes
his animal and his human form alternately throughout this
episode.

It should be evident that, speaking prosaically, the two
old men who guide and counsel Nicho, even the one he met
at Moncha's inn, are figments of his imagination, or to put
it more accurately, they are projections of his unconscious—
although Asturias relates the whole matter from Nicho's
point of view and, therefore, as if it were straight fact. The
circumstances under which he first saw the old man at Moncha's
(he was compulsively talking to Jazmín as if the dog were a
human being), lead quite naturally from the world of outward
reality to the world of psychic experience. The two old men
are but outgrowths of Jazmín, to whom they are linked by
the circumstance of their black hands, evolved from the dog's
black forepaws. In the patio, Nicho's craving for help was so
great that he turned to his dog whom his necessity soon transformed into a person. Besides, the first man disappeared with
the dog and is to that extent further identified with it. [4]

Indications that Nicho is plunging into the unconscious
begin from the moment he leaves San Miguel. The road is
soggy and full of puddles, and when he reaches Tres Aguas
(Three Waters), the hamlet where Moncha lives, the main
thoroughfare is said to be more like a river than a street.
Water is the commonest symbol of the unconscious. As with
Miguel Cara de Angel, whose return into the presence of the
President was accompanied by watery sensations indicating
his return to the womb, so it is with Nicho. Not that Moncha
is an imagined figure any more than the President was—both
have objective reality in the novel—but in Tres Aguas the

protagonist is beginning a descent into the unconscious which culminates in the cave episode.

After further strange experiences, Nicho leaves the cave in his human form and flees to the Atlantic coast, although in coyote form he remains with his mentor, Seven-year Stag, who continues to instruct him in the wisdom of the race. In a little seaport where he hides out from the postal authorities, Nicho gets a job in a hotel run by a woman called la Doña (the Lady). Offshore is the island fortress where Goyo Yic is imprisoned. They never meet, but one day Nicho does run into Goyo's wife, María Tecún, whose name he knows well because of a legend that had grown up around her.

When it become known in San Miguel that the mail had gone out with Nicho, one of the leading citizens, a Bavarian merchant, excoriates the postal clerk for employing an unsafe carrier; his doubts about Nicho spread and the town storms the post office. The general concern stems from the legend of María Tecún, according to which María Tecún was a runaway wife who had drawn her husband to his death. Her voice lured him toward mountain peaks, calling to him, and when she finally showed herself across a precipice, he fell into it attempting to reach her. She had become identified with a mountain crag that stood over a precipice and was located along the misty pass over which the highway to the capital led. It was believed that if any man whose wife had left him went near that crag, he would hear a voice coming from it and be lured into the void. Nicho's road led him by that crag. Not that the villagers cared about Nicho, but about their mail. The practical German merchant, Deferic, saved the day. With Teutonic understanding of myths and their power, he hired a muleteer to overtake Nicho and accompany him past the danger spot. To his wife, who argued that it was only a legend and nothing to worry about, Deferic explained that people sacrifice themselves to their legends; the gods have disappeared, he told her, but the legends remain, and these, like those, demand human sacrifice.

Hilario, the muleteer, travels all night, reaching Moncha's inn at dawn, where, without dismounting, he stops to chat with the old lady. She says that Nicho left a short time ago; she too has misgivings about him being able to pass the crag. Hilario continues his trip, reaches the pass without any sign of the courier, and follows on to the main post office where he learns that Nicho is officially listed as missing. The main plot therefore consists of two trips, Nicho's and Hilario's.

I   *Mediterranean Myths*

A. *Dionysus*. Looking closely at the text of this novel, we find that Asturias is writing on two levels of meaning simultaneously, following the method he used in *El Señor Presidente*. In this case he gives parallel versions of similar fertility myths, myths of death and rebirth, which will serve to emphasize some of the principal topics of the novel. The first myth portrayed by Nicho is that of Dionysus. To begin with, Nicho is a nickname for Dionisio (Dennis or Dionysus).

When the mail carrier discovers that his wife is gone, he heads for the Cuevas tavern carrying the red silk shawl which the tavern mistress likes so much. As soon as Nicho falls asleep on the floor, she attempts to steal it, but try as she may, she cannot pull the cloth away from him. He begins to revive and to mutter, over his *dead body* will she get it (*primero muerto*)! Whereupon in a frenzy she tries to *deaden* him with more liquor. Pushing a funnel into his mouth, and causing his lips to *bleed*, she pours a bottle of low-grade alcohol down his throat, tugging all the while at the shawl. All this is to no avail because, although Nicho tries to defend himself, it seems he would rather choke to death than let his precious red shawl be *torn* from him.

This scene re-enacts a major aspect of the winter Dionysia or Bacchanalia, the ritual in which Dionysus was believed to become incarnate in certain wild beasts; the beasts were captured and literally *torn* to shreds by ecstatic devotees wishing to partake of their flesh while they were alive and still possessed of the divine presence. In the tavern incident Nicho takes the part of Dionysus, Aleja Cuevas is a frenzied maenad, and the shawl is a bloody piece of his *divine* flesh which she is trying to *tear* off and consume *alive*. As the text indicates, the *blood-red* glow of the silk holds the girl's eye and strikes her as being simply *divine*. The color seems even more *alive* when the sunlight falls on it.[5]

Before the alcohol can take effect on Nicho, her scheme is spoiled by the arrival of Hilario and others, friends of Nicho, who become alarmed at his condition. His pulse is barely perceptible and he has turned cold; his shawl is *torn* and *blood*stained and his mouth bleeding. "They say there is a god who protects drunkards!" someone exclaims; "it looks as if he was even trying to eat his shawl!" (pp. 156, 157). Dionysus is also, of course, the god of drunkards, and the suggestion that anyone might "eat" the shawl is additional confirmation of what Asturias had in mind. Figuratively, therefore, Nicho has died at the hands of Aleja, just as the Dionysus animal was torn to death at the hands of the maenads.

Other details confirm this interpretation. For example, Dionysus, like most fertility gods, was associated with *serpents*, symbols of rebirth; he was known for his *facial beauty*; and his function toward the Mother Goddess was to act as a *drone* toward the queen bee. Each of these items is brought out in the text. Nicho's laugh sounds like the "rattle of a *snake*"; his features are referred to sarcastically by Aleja: it wasn't for his *pretty face* (*linda cara*) that she was listening to his drunken mumblings; and later she shouted at him: "You big *drone!*" ("*¡zanganote!*") (p. 154).

When Nicho first ordered his drinks Aleja asked him what fiesta he was celebrating. Not a fiesta, he sighed in reply, but a wake. He was referring to his sorrow over the loss of his wife, Isaura, but a wake is precisely what the winter Dionysia was, a lament for the dying fertility god and for the passing vegetation. Furthermore, Isaura represents Persephone. This goddess had suddenly vanished from the face of the earth in the same manner as Isaura. While Persephone was walking in a field the earth opened at her feet and she was carried off by Hades (Pluto) to be his wife. Thereafter she spent part of the year with her mother, Demeter, in the upper world, during which time the vegetation prospered, and part of the year with Pluto when it was wintertime. Her passing has, therefore, the same functional value as the Dionysia, and the double wake Nicho is celebrating is both his wife's and his own. "It's not a fiesta, but a wake ... come, drink with me," Nicho went on philosophically. "Caramba, it can't always be harvest time!"[6]

B. *Attis*. When the distracted letter carrier wandered off the highway into the beautiful cave and met the sorcerer Seven-year Stag, he explained: "I am looking for my wife." "The whole world is looking for her with you," retorted the Curandero, "but first we must destroy what you are carrying in those bags" (p. 245). Duty of office caused Nicho to shrink back, protecting his two bags of letters as if they were part of his own flesh.

The yearning to find his wife, however, was greater than any other consideration; inevitably he surrendered the contents of the bags to be burned. In consenting to the destruction of the mailbags for the sake of his wife, Nicho was submitting to a symbolic castration, which was the major event of another fertility ceremonial, *dies sanguinis* of the Cybele-Attis ritual. This commemorated the mutilation of young Attis for the sake of Cybele and was the functional equivalent of Dionysus' yearly death. Attis, like Tammuz, Osiris, and in Guatemala Hunahpú, was a corn god and the personification of that plant; he died in order to be reborn. When Nicho told the Curandero that he was looking for his wife (Persephone), he was saying in effect I am searching for springtime, for fertility, for the return of fruitfulness. To which the sorcerer answered: You are not alone, the whole world seeks fertility too. Then, referring to the bags: But first the seed must be destroyed, for the order of nature is that the grain should die before it germinates (Compare John 12:24, "Unless the grain of wheat falling into the ground die. . . .")

Nicho is therefore impersonating Attis here; this is substantiated by his full name, "Di-oni-si-o Aqui-no Co-jay," so spelled to illustrate someone's poor reading ability. This can be understood as, *Aquí no coj(ones) hay*: no testicles here.

The beautiful grotto in which Nicho found himself was evidentally a womb, as caves usually are in dreams, which the dark red earth at the entrance confirms; he had entered the matrix of the earth. In Greece, Delphi meant womb, and

was located partway down the slope of Mount Parnassus.
Dionysus was buried at Delphi. Nicho's presence here would
therefore represent Dionysus at Delphi in winter, during the
germination cycle associated with his worship there.

Nicho himself seems to have undergone a second figurative
death when he fell into the ravine and entered the cave. He
had been escorted there by a dog, which is the companion of
the dead; after his fall it is said that time no longer was to
count for him, and a raven, pecking at him, was surprised to
find him alive. It was love for his wife that had led him to
the cave and his entrance into it was in a sense his *Liebestod*;
it dramatized his death wish or his return to the womb. The
yearning of young fertility gods (like himself) for the Great
Mother (his wife) is interpreted as the ego's tendency to dis-
solve back into unconsciousness because the Great Mother is
a projection of the unconscious into which consciousness
seeks to be dissolved when faced with crisis.

On the level of Maya mythology the god Hunahpú stands
for the sacred corn and the sun, which go underground in
preparation for rebirth: Nicho's cave experience reproduces
this. The coyote, his *nahual*, is one of the animals who discovered
corn, and it is also an ancient sun god.

Just as Nicho reflects the essential traits of several young
fertility gods, so Isaura Terrón, his wife, is an amalgam of
goddesses of related functions. Asturias accomplishes this by
his careful choice of names. Isaura's maiden name, Terrón
(lump of earth) corroborates her relationship with Persephone
and Demeter who were earth deities. The author draws our
attention to the literal meaning of her name; *terrón* can also
mean lump of sugar, and Nicho calls her his lump of sweet
stuff ("terrón de cosa dulce," p. 152). As for her given name,
Isaura, on the one hand it recalls Isauria, that region where
the Great Mother Cybele originated; on the other, it suggests
yet another Mediterranean fertility goddess, *dea Syria*, a
title corrupted by popular usage into *Iasura*.

The concept of rebirth and regeneration deriving from the
fertility rites became the core of mystery religions; it promised
man life after death, a higher life to which he could be reborn
through rites of initiation. This aspect of the Attis-Cybele

religion was called the *taurobolium*, and we find a disguised description of it in Nicho's account of his torments over the disappearance of his wife: "I would feel jealousy coagulate in my head like big clots of thick, purple blood, which after filling me to overflowing, would spill over my face in a warm trickle and then, turning cold, would stick to my skin like cancerous scabs" (p. 256). The neophyte for whom the *taurobolium* was performed underwent a similar experience, although in his case blood did in fact flow over him: he descended into a pit under a perforated platform upon which a bull was sacrificed. As the thick, warm blood spread over his head and ran down his face, he felt that he was being reborn to a new life.

The subject of rebirth is also handled with irony: entering a village that was being harassed by Gaspar's men, Colonel Godoy tells the band that comes to welcome him with a serenade that they should compose a new piece and call it "Born Again" (*Nací de nuevo*) because up to the moment he and his detachment had arrived to protect them, they had been as good as dead! (p. 16).

C. *Venus and Adonis*. The next myth we recognize in *Hombres de maíz* is that of Venus and Adonis. Venus or Aphrodite was closely associated with the sea, born of sea foam and carried ashore on a sea shell. In Syria she was worshiped in the form of a maiden terminating in a fish; there she was known as Baalat, meaning, the Lady. The name of Nicho's employer at the seaside hotel, la Doña, means "the Lady". Her hotel is drenched in sea spray; the mosquito nettings looked like fishnets; she herself was once described as dripping with salt water, and the town reeked of salt and fish. The only guest at the hotel was a mysterious Belgian, la Doña's lover. One night during a storm he was caught at sea and drowned. The poor woman went out of her mind. Wild cries issued from her room. Nicho went in and found her sitting in bed, *stripped to the waist*, looking like an old, *disheveled mermaid*. The mourning of la Doña reproduces that of Aphrodite at the death of Adonis and that of her devotees who mimicked her sorrow at the *Adonia* festival. Annually, an effigy corpse of the god was committed to the waves amid the cries of women mourners who, with *streaming hair* and *bared breasts*, gave themselves over to transports of grief. The effigy of Adonis is depicted in the novel by the humanized tree trunks washed ashore after the storm; bobbing around with their roots, they looked like drowned men with their shoes on.

As for the blond Belgian, he fulfills the role of the departed Adonis insofar as his death is dramatically lamented by his mistress, but at the same time he also represents an earlier lover of Aphrodite, Hermes. We know this from three unmistakable tokens that he left behind in his room: a pair of slippers, a ten-gallon hat, and a candle; the familiar symbols of Hermes are his sandals, his broadbrim hat, and the torch by which he escorted souls to Hades. Nicho succeeded the lamented one in the affections of la Doña, taking over the role of the resurrected Adonis who returned to Aphrodite in the spring. The effeminate beauty of this god is portrayed by another character, Juliantico, a young ferry man who had hair like combed flax and the eyes of an infant god ("ojos de Niño Dios", p. 272).

Inasmuch as Asturias has been sketching a survey of Mediterranean vegetation gods, perhaps the name Julian, introducing a new and unessential character at the end of the novel is intended to suggest Julian the Apostate, the emperor who made the last attempt to reinstate pagan worship. He conceived of a syncretic Baal, *Sol Invictus*, in whom each worshiper was to see his respective god: Attis, Bacchus, or Adonis. As for the Great Goddesses, they had slipped from their supreme position, succumbing to ever increasing male predominance.

The same happened to la Doña. She died and left Nicho in sole possession of the hotel, like the syncretic Baal bereft of his Baalat. Our last glimpse of Nicho shows his decline, corresponding to the final status of fertility gods in the West. As he grew old, Nicho's face twisted to one side; his jaw dropped and his open mouth tended to attract flies. They crawled right in and he had to spit them out. The visual impression of this distorted head crawling with flies brings to mind Beelzebub, Lord of the Flies, who was originally a Baal, a Canaanite fertility god. If Nicho is now Beelzebub, then to Jews and Christians he is the Adversary. Likewise Dionysus, the Attic goat god with cleft hoofs and horns, came to personify Satan, following the time-honored pattern whereby the gods of one age become the demons of the next. In *El Señor Presidente* Asturias associated Miguel/Tammuz with Satan, too.

II   *Aztec Myths*

A. *Huitzilopochtli*. Many characters besides Nicho depict fertility myths and rituals. Several gods from the Aztec pantheon are discernible in the first section. Gaspar Ilóm, whose name (jaspar) recalls that green stones symbolized both corn and the sun to American Indians, is Huitzilopochtli, the sun and fertility god; his wife, la Piojosa Grande (literally, the Great Filthy One), is the Great Earth Mother, Tlazolteotl, whose name in Nahuatl means "Goddess of Filth." From their union was born Martín who is actually referred to as corn in the novel—not an unusual analogy in view of the Indians' belief that they were Corn Men. We see here a repetition of the archetype: the Great Mother whose son is identified with her lover, both being personifications of corn. As solar god, Gaspar brought himself back to life: poisoned the night of the fiesta, he cleansed himself in the river and "reappeared with the dawn," like the sun (p. 25).

B. *Quetzalcoatl*. Another Mexican myth of rebirth is that of the rain and fertility god Quetzalcoatl, better known as the Plumed Serpent. He had a twin, Xolotl, and together they represented the planet Venus in its dual aspect of morning and evening star. As the myth in question is simpler than most, it is given here to demonstrate Asturias' method. The Machojóns, Señor Tomás and his son, impersonate the divine twins: Thomas means twin; Machojón is the augmentative of viril, reproductive. Old Tomás and his wife were the traitors who had taken the poison to Gaspar. Later Señor Tomás blamed her for the betrayal and for bringing on the curse whereby young Machojón disappeared on his way to visit his sweetheart and left no trace. It was said that he became a wandering star. Some people claimed they could see him in the brush fires: he would go galloping through the flames waving his big Mexican hat. They said he was clothed in gold and his face looked like a statue with glass eyes. Venus is a "wandering star"; it shines like gold on the tropical horizon. The serpent heads of Quetzalcoatl, like those at Teotihuacán, often had eyes of obsidian glass.

Old Tomás would hurry off to every brush fire, yearning for a glimpse of his son. He never did see him, but the *maiceros* always told him that they did because that way they fooled him into turning over more and more of his land for their use. The more fires there were, the more chance he had of seeing his boy again; he cared about nothing else. One night, months later, when the corn was dry and ready for storage, he donned his son's clothes and wide hat, and led a mule out to the corn fields. He set fire to the corn and began galloping through the flames. As he rode he examined his hand and clothing and saw with satisfaction that they were all gold, like Machojón's. He wanted to look like his son, and he did: nobody seeing him could have told them apart. What old Machojón had done was to set fire to himself. He died in the blaze along with his wife and many others. Likewise, Quetzalcoatl immolated himself on a pyre, and his body rose from the ashes into the sky where it became the morning star. Identified as old Tomás was with his son, we can see that their combined experiences reproduce the essentials of this particular myth.

While on earth Quetzalcoatl reigned happily in Tulán, but he was led into temptation by Xochiquetzal and sinned with her. She was the goddess of spring, another Persephone. Like Adonis, Tammuz, and others, not to forget Señor Tomás himself, the god's woes were brought about by a woman, the Great Mother. He left Tulán, and accompanied by his dwarfish attendants (for he was the patron of dwarfs), he departed for the mythical city, Tlillán Tlapallán, "the place of conflagration," where he was to die. Resting along the way, he marked the spot by transfixing one tree with another in the shape of a cross. Machojón's parallel actions are as follows: before setting fire to the fields, he had visited them accompanied by his godson, a dwarf. Together they had laughed at the scarecrows they saw: two poles in the shape of a cross surmounted by a Mexican hat ("dos palos en cruz": *palo* means either pole or tree; the emphasis on the Mexican hat underscores that it is a Mexican myth; p. 41). Then thinking of the fire he was planning, old Tomás imagined the funereal bells that would toll "Tilán-tilón-tilán-tilón. . ." after the conflagration.

There is more. In the novel during a long drought, the despairing *maiceros* began to fear it was a punishment for having hoaxed Señor Tomás. They thought it might help if they would go and kneel before him and confess the wrong they had done him—just so long as it would rain. Clearly the old man is in the position of a rain god. Besides, he was a heavy smoker, as all rain gods are in Central America, for that is how clouds are made.

C. *The Great Mother.* The sacrifice of the entire Zacatón family by decapitation was carried out by the Tecún brothers as part of a sorcery to relieve old Yaca their mother of a bad case of hiccoughs. A counterpart of Tlazolteotl is the old earth and corn mother, Toci, "Our Grandmother." The Tecún boys call Yaca, "mi nana," which means indifferently mother or grandma; her hiccoughs probably represent an earthquake. In honor of Toci Aztec women were beheaded to signify the plucking of corn ears. This sacrificial rite is conveyed by the eight heads of the Zacatóns which the Tecún brothers brought home and presented to Yaca (the shock did cure her hiccoughs). Corn is one of the big grasses, and that is what the word *zacatón* means, big grass. Asturias hints as much: "they decapitated the Zacatóns, who were cut down like grass" ("Decapitaron a los Zacatón, que fueron arrancados de la vida como cortar zacate," p. 255). Moreover, the name of Yaca Tecún recalls Yacatecutli, a variant of Quetzalcoatl, so that in her person the Supreme Pair are combined.

III　*Other Myths*

A. *Demeter and Persephone.* In broad outline, the second section of the novel illustrates the Demeter-Persephone fertility myth once more, though from another aspect. Goyo Yic, the husband of María Tecún, had been a mother to her having brought her up from babyhood. When she disappeared he cursed her angrily: "Hija de puerca" ("child of a pig," p. 93) but he yearned for her just the same and spent years searching for her. In the end they were reunited, but in the meantime María had married another man, thinking Goyo was dead. In his travels through the mountains of Guatemala searching for María, Goyo is like the Great Mother Demeter who wandered through the world searching for her daughter Persephone. María is like Persephone who married Pluto because María's second husband was reputed to have a pact with the devil, and this connection would identify him as Pluto, Lord of the underworld. Persephone (María) may rightly be called "child of a pig" because her mother, Demeter, was originally a sow goddess. Goyo is also identified with the Great Mother through his opossum, as this animal is a Maya symbol of the feminine capacity.

B. *Isis and Osiris.* The myth of Isis and Osiris is found in the anecdote of O'Neill and Miguelita, in the third section. Osiris, Egyptian god of fertility, was the personification of the Nile (Greek: *Neilos*, Spanish, *Nilo*). The gringo O'Neill, known locally as *Neil* or *Nelo*, had been a sewing–machine salesman who passed through San Miguel Acatán. Hilario, the muleteer who was sent to catch up with Nicho, remembered O'Neill from childhood, and as he was the village raconteur when he was in his cups, he had made up a romantic tale concerning him. The story grew each time Hilario was at the tavern as he "remembered" some more of it; the townsfolk firmly believed him.

It seems that O'Neill *idol*ized Miguelita but, rejected by her, he left Acatán in despair saying he would *throw himself into the sea* (as the Nile does) and become a drunken sailor (Osiris was the god of wine). Miguelita, a girl invented by Hilario (or so he thinks), was an industrious seamstress; the whirr of her sewing machine had been a familiar sound to the villagers, and, according to popular belief, it could still be heard on certain nights at the stroke of twelve. As O'Neill is Osiris, so Miguelita is Isis. The Egyptian goddess invented weaving, according to Plutarch, and like all Great Mothers, she spun the threads of men's destiny and wove the fabric of their lives. Hilario asserts that since the advent of sewing machines, the spool has replaced the spindle; we may take this to mean that Miguelita's machine replaces the symbolic loom and spinning wheel of the Great Mother. As weaving by the goddess stands for the passage of time, it is appropriate that the whirr of the sewing machine should be heard at the stroke of midnight, the end of another day.

When Hilario stopped to chat with old Moncha on his way to the capital and they discussed the danger of the legend of María Tecún for poor Nicho, he remarked that there was probably no more truth to it than there was to the legend of Miguelita, which he had made up when he was drunk. Wise old Moncha (her name, Ramona, from Raymond, means wise) explained to him that he may have thought he invented Miguelita, but he did not; he only *remembered* her; that in his drunkenness he had drawn Miguelita out of the memory that his ancestors had left in his blood, and that if *he* had not remembered her, someone else would have. This is a folksy way of saying that Miguelita originated from the collective unconscious which each of us inherits from the dim, ancestral past, according to Jung. Hilario's drunkenness when he told his legend shows that it did indeed issue from the unconscious. Moncha is saying that myths are "true" when they correspond to some inner necessity of a group (someone else would have remembered Miguelita if Hilario had not), when they yield a meaning with which a people can identify. Such is also the opinion of the mythologist, Mircea Eliade.[7] The truth of legends depends not on facts, which the popular mind distorts as necessary, but on the psychic need they fill. Asturias has illustrated this distortion by giving us the true story of María Tecún and the legend that developed from it.

The question arises, why was the story thus distorted? What psychic need did the legend fill?

CHAPTER 5

The Quest for the Feminine

THE text of *Hombres de maíz* undoubtedly contains other myths besides those outlined in the previous chapter, and, owing to the basic similarity between the myths of all peoples, some passages allow for more than one interpretation, providing further mythic allusions. It stands to reason that Asturias has a purpose in juxtaposing these many parallel versions of fertility myths with his narrative. In the first place, they support a major topic of the book, fertility. Furthermore, by relating the present with antiquity, they mark the continuity and immutability of human aspirations.

There is another important aspect about them, however. Myths are a source of knowledge about man's psyche because, like dreams, they are dictated by the unconscious (in this case the collective unconscious) expressing itself in symbols or archetypes. According to Jungian psychology, one of the principal constituents of mythology is a series of archetypes standing in organic relation to the stages of the growth of consciousness, both in man as an individual and as a collectivity. In other words, mythology can be read as a record of human development. Such appears to be the use Asturias makes of his myths, and with this reading, the unity of the novel becomes evident, its pattern clear and simple.

Nicho is the central figure; the process of his psychic evolution, told in the third section, is the heart of the matter, and most of the secondary characters are related to this in one way or another. Instead of electing straight Maya mythology to illustrate Nicho's experiences, the author has created within the framework of Maya culture, a system of local legends which, as far as Nicho is concerned, serve his personal, individual needs. At the same time, the legends are in themselves valid fictional entities, in the sense that the Oedipus myth is a good story regardless of what psychological value it may also contain. These are the substance of the first two sections. It will be useful to go over that part of the novel again.

The manner, tone, and much of the subject of the first section point back to the origins of the highland Mayas, reproducing the mentality of those times. Using the Raynaud version of *The Annals of the Cakchiquels*, which he and a friend translated into Spanish, Asturias transcribes some of its sonorous and descriptive names and carries on some of its legends. For example, one Cakchiquel tradition tells of two heroes, the chieftain Volcán and the warrior White Hummingbird, who subdued a great fire by capturing the Fire Spirit and imprisoning it; upon returning with their captive to the waiting tribes, they warned that, if the Fire Spirit were ever freed from its bonds, the conflagration would break out again. The oracle is fulfilled in *Hombres de maíz*. Fire breaks out in the mountains of Ilóm through the fault of the *maiceros* who burn down vast forests of precious woods in order to clear the land for their corn fields. Like White Hummingbird of old, the cacique Gaspar succeeds in mastering the fire by his guerrilla war against the invaders: "Gaspar Ilóm, the intrepid warrior, had captured the fire which was running loose in the mountains, taken it home and tied it to his door so that it could do no harm" (p. 45). But the hero was betrayed and his men slaughtered. The Fire Spirit escaped once more and none was left to resist its destruction. Fires began again to ravage the mountainsides when the *maiceros* resumed their burnings; countless lives were destroyed in the holocausts of Machojón and Godoy. The mountains of Ilóm were ravaged and came to be known as the Site of Maledictions.

The cause of this devastation is the curse laid by the legendary Brujos de las Luciérnagas. To judge from their lineage, these sorcerers were fire spirits and powerful magicians in charge of guarding the mountains of Ilóm. They were identified with ancient deities of Cakchiquel lore named Entrechocadores de Pedernales ("Those Who Strike Flints Together"). In *The Annals of the Cakchiquels*, a demigod bearing this name was characterized as a killer and a thief who demanded propitiation of blood-colored garments. He appears to have been a sacrificer, inasmuch as in the sacred scriptures of both Cakchiquel and Quiché Mayas this office was linked with kidnapping or stealing: sacrificers abducted their victims.

Rather than a revenge or punishment it would seem that the loss of lives attributed to the sorcerers should be looked upon as a grand scale sacrifice, a hecatomb performed to promote the fertility of the land. The concept of human sacrifice conforms more closely with the primitive mentality evoked in the first part of the novel than does the somewhat sophisticated idea of revenge. This becomes clearer in the third section when Nicho discusses the matter with the old man he met at Moncha's, as we shall see. And this grand scale sacrifice is to become part of the mythological apparatus of later characters, especially Nicho's.

In short, the entire first section may be looked upon as an account of mythical events. Undoubtedly a rebellion of Indians did occur and was put down: years later María Tecún spoke of it as some Indian massacre or other (p. 270); but even for those who lived through the events, men like the soldier Benito Ramos who served under Godoy, the memory of them became overlaid with the supernatural. Whatever it was that actually took place, the material Asturias presents is already largely distorted by the popular mind and molded to the Maya world view, in the manner that the legend of María Tecún distorted the tale of Goyo Yic and his wife.

I *Sacrifice*

Sacrifice is discussed on two subsequent occasions in connection with Nicho. The German, Deferic, who sent Hilario to overtake him, said that legends had replaced the gods, but that like the gods, they exacted their toll of human sacrifice.

Before anyone could catch up with him, Nicho turned off the highway with the man who led him to the cave. They had talked about the same subject as Deferic, but from another point of view. Referring to the sorcerers' curse and desolation brought on by the *maiceros*, the old man explained that the

Earth, like any other mother, brings forth the corn at the price of pain and labor. Therefore, she needs sustenance. Where she used to receive bones, the bones of ancestors, nowadays corn growers give her nothing. They leave her empty. It was for this reason, he said, that the *maiceros* had been cursed. That which they would not give freely was taken from them. They were visited with death because the Earth demands bones for her nourishment.

Like most agrarian primitives, American Indians offered ritual sacrifices designed to guarantee the fertility of the earth. In a profound way fertility is bound to destruction and cannot dispense with it, as was seen in *El Señor Presidente*. Man's universal experience is that growth and fruitfulness spring from death. "The bones of ancestors" refer, therefore, to human victims formerly sacrificed and probably buried right in the corn fields. At any rate, sacrifices were "demanded" and received by rain and earth gods. But the *maiceros* performed no ritual, no sacrifice; they took from the earth and gave nothing back. To the Indian mind this upset the balance of nature. Therefore, a catastrophe like either of the big fires was understood to be the means by which this balance was restored—because to people who live close to nature, things do not happen by accident, or as we would say, from natural causes, but by design or from supernatural causes. (This supernatural design is generally the basis of legends that gives them their psychological truth.) The function of the imaginary sorcerers and their curse was to give form, as it were, to the supernatural design by which the mountains of Ilóm were ravaged.

But, it may be objected, we agreed that the man with whom Nicho discussed these matters is not a real person at all but a projection of his unconscious. Is it, therefore, not unlikely that a subject as remote from his personal preoccupations as an old legend about corn growers, should fill his mind at this moment? No, on the contrary, and for two reasons. First, legends and myths, which ordinarily lie dormant beneath the level of consciousness, tend to be activated in times of crisis. The contents of the collective unconscious surge to consciousness in dreams, hallucinations, or obsessions—indeed, the unconscious can best communicate its messages this way; for this reason the dreams of patients undergoing analysis are richer than at other times. The fact that this legend is independent of Nicho's conscious problems indicates that it comes from the collective unconscious. Second, this particular legend has to do with sacrifice, and he is preparing for sacrifice at this moment, although unwittingly. Sacrifice is the basis of all rebirth rituals and of all psychic development; it is a form of death without which there can be no rebirth, no resurrection, no renewal, and it is the only way for Nicho to regain peace of mind. The old man is an archetype of meaning, and his function is to clarify the meaning of sacrifice for Nicho.

According to Jung, sacrifice is an instinctive process of transformation by which one gives up something valuable in order to get it back in a renewed form. Thus, when a man performs sacrifice he gives up part of his libido (psychic energy) to the unconscious; as a result, he experiences a release of psychic energy which renews him.[1] We shall return to the question of sacrifice presently. In the meantime we can share Deferic's understanding of legends and the blind force that impels a man to sacrifice himself for them.

II *Rebirth and the Great Mother*

The basic pattern of all the myths in *Hombres de maíz*, whichever deity they concern, is the experience of death and rebirth. Central to each myth is the Great Mother goddess. Rebirth and the Great Mother: in these two primordial archetypes we have the keys to the meaning and coherence of this sprawling novel.

Rebirth is always a symbol of psychic transformation. The fertility rites, which were celebrated ostensibly to make the Earth Mother fruitful by sacrificing representatives of the vegetation gods, were a form of rebirth; they had the psychological benefit of assisting in the development of consciousness. From the state of unconsciousness in which he is born, man grows to consciousness by a slow and arduous process. Annual fertility rites provided the worshiper, who identified with the dying god, with a periodic opportunity for renewal and regeneration; they sustained him in his struggle to preserve consciousness and to resist the lure of the unconscious. Essentially the lure of the unconscious is the lure of the feminine in the sense that it comprises not only woman but all that to which man instinctively attributes the feminine capacity: earth, matter, night and darkness, the underworld, the yawning pit, the unconscious, and death. (Conversely, sky, spirit, light and day, and consciousness belong to the masculine capacity.) The feminine in its widest sense is personified in the primordial figure of the Great Mother, which can appear at once good and terrible.

To meet the successive needs of a lifelong effort to expand consciousness, many modifications of the basic death-and-rebirth patterns have developed. In the dragon fight, the hero risks death (this is the sacrifice) in order to kill a monster (the Terrible Mother) and rescue a damsel (the helpful aspect of the unconscious); then he marries her (rebirth to a new life). This is interpreted as a means to strengthen the ego by differentiation, that is, by freeing the personal soul image (called anima by Jung) from the devouring aspect of the unconscious. It is a stage in human development, one that Cara de Angel, for instance, seemed to have reached but from which he later regressed.

This transpersonal experience makes its appearance in *Hombres de maíz* in an allusion to the Minotaur: to the priest of San Miguel, worried about the detrimental effect of the María Tecún crag upon his flock, the counsel was given by a learned colleague to read the legend of the Minotaur (probably the only direct reference to a Greek myth in the novel). Theseus' adventure is a typical dragon fight and follows the rebirth pattern. He braved the labyrinth, slew the monstrous Minotaur who like the Tecún crag fed on human victims, and ran off with Ariadne. Generally, the damsel is a captive of the beast, but in this case she already had the positive role of helpmate; she is the anima, while the Minotaur and its labyrinth are the unconscious.

The learned colleague was right: the dragon fight is the psychological answer to the problem of the Tecún legend. Both the crag and the Minotaur, by whom men allow themselves to be overpowered, are symbols of uncontrollable instincts (the Terrible Mother) which consciousness must master lest it be swallowed by them. For "abandoned husbands" to whom the crag personifies the destruction of the ego, the example of Theseus is precisely what is needed to exorcise it because it embodies the necessary ingredients of sacrifice and renewal.

III *Death and Rebirth of Nicho: His Journey Through the Cave*

Another version of the rebirth myth is the night sea journey or descent into the underworld, according to which the hero, as a figure of the sun, is swallowed by a monster in the west and disgorged in the east, strengthened and wiser. The myth is connected with passage into the second half of life, whereas the dragon fight is associated with initiation from childhood into manhood. Passage into the second part of life is a process of self-realization which Jung calls individuation.[2]

Nicho's journey through the cave marks his symbolic death and resurrection. There was a question whether he was dead or alive when he fell down the mountainside. After taking his first steps into the mouth of the cave, he stopped and looked back over his shoulder because he felt as if he were entering the gullet of some animal that might snap its jaws and swallow him. But the desire to find his wife overcame his apprehension. In other words, his wife, who was his anima, guided him in this dangerous step. When he reached the grotto the sorcerer informed him: "You have been traveling Westward, and now you are headed toward the openings" (p. 245) *desembocaduras*, openings, suggest a disgorging). Having therefore entered the cave in the west, Nicho was crossing beneath the mountains, in the path the sun appears to follow in its nightly course, and would eventually emerge in the east, as his subsequent flight to the Atlantic coast indicates.

In the archetypal journey, the hero generally gets hungry and lights a fire, which indicates the reawakening of consciousness; then he eats some of the monster's heart, which helps him discover the meaning of his journey. In Nicho's case, a fire is lighted to burn his mailbags, whereby he learns the fate of Isaura and accepts it: this means he conquered the dangerous lure of the feminine. He is hungry and he sees others eating products of the earth's matrix, which are comparable in symbolic import to the monster's heart.

Under the aegis of the Curandero, Nicho was initiated into the values and wisdom of his culture. It is characteristic of the individuation process that the initiate is his own teacher. So is Nicho. He submits to the guidance of the Curandero, who, as another wise old man archetype, is a personification of the source of our psychic being, the Self. When the archetypal hero emerges from his underworld ordeal, he is victorious, like the sun at dawn: *Sol Invictus*. We saw that Nicho represented this syncretic god too. Having recovered his equilibrium concerning his wife, he was able to begin the second part of life with composure. At the Hotel King he became "a nobody, but a great nobody" (p. 272). In Jungian psychology, the most important task a man can accomplish is to achieve inner equilibrium through self-realization. Outwardly the results are not visible: Nicho was a nobody—his greatness rested on his inner growth.

IV   *Abandoned Husbands*

In the early stage of ego consciousness, the feminine components in man are deliberately suppressed and the masculine promoted. They do not disappear, of course; they merely sink into the unconscious, clustering around the soul image or anima. An illustration of the process whereby the ego is developed through suppression of feminine elements occurs toward the end of *Hombres de maíz*. In Goyo's island prison, an ancient fortress dating back to Colonial days, there was an old sign saying: "NO TALK ABOUT WOMEN ALLOWED." In the *heroic* days of the castle, says the text, whoever broke this rule was thrown to the sharks. Discussing this with another prisoner, Goyo wonders if the sign applied to mothers: "Mothers more than any other women!" exclaims the other; "nothing so weakens a soldier as talking about his mother; he ceases to be a man and becomes a little child" (p. 260; loose translation).

The subject is not so odd when transferred to the psychological plane and to the *heroic* stage of ego formation, where consciousness is struggling to disengage itself from the Great Mother. In order to survive, it must sever decisively with all femininity; to break the rule means to be engulfed in the Terrible Mother (i.e, to regress) of which the sea and sharks are vivid figures.

A man generally experiences his anima through the woman he loves or through an idealized figure such as Hilario's "Miguelita." In the individuation process he must withdraw the projection and recognize it for what it is, his own feminine components. The prominence of woman in *Hombres de maíz* is unmistakable. Woman dominates the novel by her *absence*, and it can be read as a quest for the feminine—for the missing half.

This is seen in Goyo and Nicho's search for their vanished partners and in Hilario's ideal of a "Miguelita," which to him was more real and more precious than the flesh-and-blood Aleja Cuevas he was about to marry. All three men are obsessed by a vision of woman that has no counterpart in objective reality. We understand this when Goyo, having regained his sight, finally does see his wife, who is an ordinary woman after all. They are really pursuing an inner vision which they have projected upon María, Isaura, and "Miguelita," respectively. On the myth level each of the three women in question is a figure of the Great Mother, as we have seen, which indicates that this is the archetype the men have projected upon them.

The significance of this recurring figure, the Great Mother, is further clarified in the course of Hilario's trip over the María Tecún Pass when he was trying to catch up with Nicho. As the muleteer approached the famous crag said to call to abandoned husbands, he too heard a voice, but it was not calling him. It was the voice of the now legendary blind man Goyo, calling "María Tecún!" He covered his ears but he still heard it, and he realized that it was coming from within himself: "Who has not called the name of a woman who vanished into his past?" he mused, identifying himself with Goyo. "Who has not blindly pursued that being which departed from his being when he made his presence felt?" ("¿Quién no ha perseguido como ciego ese ser que se fué de su ser, cuando él se hizo presente?" (p. 189). These words seem to refer to man's own femininity which he possessed in the dawn state of psychic wholeness (at birth) and which was suppressed as he developed consciousness.[3] But that part of him which separated from him as his ego developed, or to use Asturias' terminology, as he "made his presence felt," that image of the vanished feminine is never completely lost: "Every man carries within himself an eternal image of woman"; relegated to the unconscious at an early stage of his life, it must be reactivated in a later stage if man is to regain the integrity he requires for mental health.[4]

Is not this disappearing wife, combined with the husband's idealization of her, a graphic expression of that later stage when a man's feminine components begin to be consciously felt? Withdrawing the projection of his anima (symbolized by the wife's departure), he seeks to reactivate the long suppressed part of his psyche, calling "the woman who vanished in his past." He is looking for the missing feminine who is none other than his unconscious.

V   *The María Tecún Crag: Instigator of Sacrifice*

As Hilario rode past the crag he accurately described it as the "image of absence" (p. 189). On this shapeless rock people had projected their inward vision of that "absent woman," the anima. Deferic also used the word absence in connection with it. When he said that its legend demanded sacrifice as had the gods of old, he added that the knives of obsidian which once ripped out the hearts of sacrificial victims had been replaced by knives of absence, an absence that sears and maddens ("los cuchillos de la ausencia que hiere y enloquece") (p. 181). This absence refers literally to the void left by runaway wives, but figuratively it alludes to the missing half which man needs for completion, the feminine personification of the unconscious.

The "absence that sears and maddens," of which the crag is an image, describes the psychic process by which the impulse to sacrifice is activated, for it is the Great Mother who prods

man to sacrifice. The need for sacrifice stems from the fact
that, as Jung says, "the life force wears out, turns 'bad' or
gets lost, and must be renewed at regular intervals. . . . In
the act of sacrifice the consciousness gives up its power and
possessions in the interest of the unconscious. This makes
possible a union of opposites resulting in a release of energy."
If a person neglects this bond with the uncouscious, that is,
if he omits to sacrifice to the Great Mother, she torments
him until he does, or as in the classical example of Pentheus
killed by his mother, she overpowers him by insanity or death
(sears and maddens).[5]

The crag was located on the edge of a pit and lured men
into it because the ambivalent figure it represented to them
in times of crisis sprang from the unconscious and called them
back to it: unconsciousness is dreaded as the dissolution of
individuality and desired as the state of blissful irresponsibility.
When a situation arises such as Nicho's loss, with which the
ego (conscious mind) cannot cope, help may be elicited from
the unconscious by the rite of sacrifice and renewal in one
form or another. For Nicho, we know, it was his descent into
the underworld. He stepped aside from the "road of reality"
(consciousness) which was leading him to calamity and despair,
and turning inward he drew strength from the redeeming forces
of the collective psyche. The old man who led him to the
cave talked to him about the need for sacrifice and renewal,
giving the earth as an example and alluding to the sacrifice
(or punishment as he called it) connected with the *maiceros*.
He prepared Nicho for the sacrifice to which he was leading
him.

By plunging into the cave alone (even his dog was gone by
then), Nicho was acting in the manner of Theseus entering
the labyrinth or the sun descending into the earth monster
to regenerate himself; he did not run away, as Cara de Angel
attempted to do. Inside he met, appropriately, that other
psychic projection, the descendant of Those Who Strike
Flints Together—a sacrificer. The destruction of the mailbags
by this figure, an action which graphically represents the
emasculation of Attis, confirms Nicho's sacrifice. The fire
consumed the sacrifice. From the matrix of life into which

he had boldly penetrated, Nicho drew the healing strength he needed.

In accepting the loss of his wife, he understood that there was nothing left for him but to "swallow her adored image"; through his brimming eyes "he let her drop inside his aching body" (p. 248). This is a pictorial way of expressing the fact that Nicho, who had projected his anima on his wife and then temporarily on the María Tecún crag, now withdraws the projection and takes it back into himself.

An experience parallel to Nicho's and to which Jung has frequent reference, is the well-known case of Faust. In the first part of the drama Gretchen carried the projection of Faust's anima (as Isaura did Nicho's), but when she died Faust was forced to take the projection back into himself. He then proceeded to explore the inner world of his unconscious. The world that Nicho explored was not only that of his ancestry—the collective unconscious molded and colored by the traditions peculiar to the highland Indians of Guatemala—but also his personal unconscious, where, under the symbolism of finding out about his wife and swallowing her image, he was able to reintegrate his femininity in his psyche.

The sections of the novel which cover Deferic's and the old man's ideas of sacrifice, as well as Nicho's entry into the cave, are applications and further illustrations of the material in Jung's chapter on sacrifice. It would seem to me incredible if the one was not inspired by the other. The possibility does exist, nevertheless, as Goethe's case shows, that an author could unintentionally portray these unconscious processes.

Although the great rock called María Tecún was no longer a menace to Nicho, still, he was curious to know what or who it was. In the end of the novel when he meets the real María, he learns from his mentor, Seven-year Stag, that it is not she, a mere woman, but Gaspar's wife, la Piojosa Grande, whose spirit animates the crag in the mountain pass. On the night that Gaspar was poisoned, the Curandero explains, la Piojosa Grande ran off into the dark and disappeared like water falling over a cliff; nevertheless, her body, insubstantial like air, was caught on the ledge as if paralyzed, between heaven and earth and the void, where it will remain for all time.

That night Gaspar tasted death in his cup of poison, but he was reborn in the cleansing waters of the river; his experience is another version of the initiation rite, whose purpose is to strengthen the ego by suppressing the feminine. Gaspar's wife demonstrates this graphically by vanishing into the dark. Thus Asturias asserts in still another way that the crag represents the feminine principle which, when suppressed, sinks into the unconscious like water plunging over a cliff, while a figuration of her stands, not in heaven, nor on earth, nor yet in a vacuum, but rooted forever in the human psyche.

The sorcerer says that la Piojosa Grande is María la Lluvia who holds in her arms her son and Gaspar's, the corn. Interpreted, this means that she is the rain goddess who to the Maya is Xmucané, the moon; her son, the corn, is Hunahpú, which makes Gaspar the sun. Sun and moon are, we know, the supreme gods of the Maya whose religion is based on the cultivation and deification of maize, just as the religions of ancient Mediterranean peoples were founded upon the cultivation of wheat and other cereals. In this way the novel and its characters remain anchored in Maya mythology, and the author has developed legends for them appropriate to their particular beliefs and circumstances but structured on psychological truths common to all men.

We are now in position to appreciate the import of the epigraph Asturias has chosen for his novel: "Here the woman/ I, the sleeper."[6] If we equate sleep with unconsciousness, the woman thus placed in apposition to the sleeper expresses the presence of the Eternal Feminine in man's unconscious. It is a visualization of Jung's assertion that each man carries within him the eternal image of woman. The epigraph marvelously summarizes *Hombres de maíz.*

VI   *Conclusion*

To recapitulate, the novel dramatizes the stages in the development of consciousness based on Jung's analytical psychology with Nicho Aquino as the principal character. Divided into three main sections, the first two present local events distorted into legends and myths that make up Nicho's psychological equipment; his adventures in the third section show the application of this mythological material to his personal problems. The classical myths portrayed in the sub-structure of the novel serve as pointers; they substantiate the psychological theme and emphasize the analogies that exist among all mythologies. Different as to detail, Nicho's myths are identical in structure and psychological function with those operating in men of all times and places.

Asturias has been quoted as saying that he is not a myth maker. Perhaps this is true in an absolute sense, but as regards his characters in *Hombres de maíz*, he has equipped them with myths and legends suitable to their condition. Myths of death and rebirth, of sacrifice and renewal that affect them, help them surmount their difficulties, and see them through their lives in the same way that "real" myths affect the real men and women in Guatemala or in any other part of the world fortunate enough to have preserved its myths.

This has been by no means as extensive an interpretation as the novel merits, but it suffices to indicate one of the themes that give it organic unity and purpose as a work of art.

CHAPTER 6

Viento fuerte

THE banana trilogy consists of the novels entitled *Viento fuerte*, *El papa verde* and *Los ojos de los enterrados* (Strong Wind, The Green Pope, The Eyes of the Buried), which in broad outline trace the effect of the United Fruit Company on the lives of the people of Guatemala. *Viento fuerte* (1950) begins in the epic times when American contractors were clearing tropical forests along the Pacific coast and constructing railroads. Workers from the highlands converged on this uninhabited area, where snakes, fevers, accidents, and stifling heat weakened the best of them. In spite of the hardships the idea that they were reclaiming lands from the jungle and opening new worlds for future crops appealed to many of them, and they were proud to take part in the grand enterprise. Besides, the determination and efficiency of the gringos inspired respect: these men knew what they were doing, and they stayed away from women.

Among the early laborers Adelaido Lucero was one of those who stayed on, married, and settled near the headquarters of the foreign company. He remained in the company's employ all his life, but for his sons he had greater ambitions. He began buying land for them from their early childhood so that they would be able to grow their own crops and be independent planters. His friend Cucho, on the other hand, was one of those who contracted tuberculosis and went back to the sierras. Cucho took with him the memory of the fertile soil and luxuriant vegetation as of a promised land. At his urging several young men from that high barren region moved down to the coast, and settling near the Luceros they eventually became independent planters, selling their banana crops to the company.

Meanwhile the company kept developing its plantations. The pioneers from the original crew had gone and were replaced by administrative personnel—by the machinery, as one of the men put it. "We are simply machines. We are stationed here, like automatons. When we're not working, we do nothing. We take no part in this magic world of flowers and birds. We don't live. See the natives? They're alive. They may be good. They may be bad. But as for us, we're neither good nor bad; we're just machines." This was how he described company administrators to his wife, Leland Foster, when she came down for a visit. "But great enterprises like this," she objected, "cannot help but be an adventure to everyone involved." "Yes," he would agree, "but the men of adventure are not those who are here now. Those men perished in the adventure, and in their place came the employees, we who live without risk or adventure, not good, not bad, not happy, not sad, simply machines."- "If so," she would argue, "if the epic and heroic days are gone altogether, then the company must already be decrepit because adventure is a sign of youth. The total adventure," she added, "would have been to create a ring of human cooperation around these plantations, a joint effort with the local people, instead of settling for the security of artificially subjecting them."[1]

This passage is one among many that foreshadows the outcome of the trilogy, for in the end, the workers will wrest from the unwilling company an agreement for cooperation.

Leland Foster came to the tropics on a vacation, but she stayed for many years. While visiting the Luceros she ran into Lester Mead, a gawky American with an ear–splitting laugh, who traveled around peddling sewing articles from house to house. People said he was the son of one of the company's pioneers. His customers thought he was a little daft and called him Cosi, probably from *coser*, to sew, mocking his accent. When he talked to Leland, she discovered that in spite of his appearance he was no fool. He spoke English in refined and measured tones. She thought that he must be an adventurer, and partly because of that she fell in love with him. She divorced Pyle and married Mead. He gave up peddling and became a planter like the young Lucero brothers and the others.

The little company town consists mostly of the peons employed to irrigate, weed, spray, and prune the endless parallel alleys of banana plants. The office workers, Americans and middle-class Guatemalans, live in separate housing, also blocked off in parallel lots. There is friction between the company and the laborers over pay, and the laborers also object to the white-collar employees. The workers have moved to the coast with their families, but their wives and daughters are constantly being victimized by the lechery of the administration staff who live singly. There are protests, gatherings, and threats. Eventually soldiers are brought in and permanently stationed in town to protect company personnel from the populace. Young Lino Lucero and his brother Juan are among the agitators, while Adelaido Lucero and his generation, the old-timers, now in minor positions of responsibility such as foremanships, try to pacify the younger folk and preach patience. Although this second generation grumbles and menaces, it takes no effective action. Not until the third generation will the question of strikes arise.

By selling their produce to the company, the independent planters prosper until the day the company cuts the price of a stem from sixty to twenty-five cents, and the planters' vaunted independence is suddenly exploded. The young men decide they had better sell the fruit anyway. All except Mead; for him it is a matter of moral principle not to comply with such injustice.

"It's pure robbery," shouts Juan Lucero, "and what's so damnable is that they are two-faced. They give out all sorts of help, they fight diseases, and when the fruit is ripe for cutting, they ruin us by refusing to buy it. They're not acting in good faith!"

"Right! However excellent the company people may be as individuals, when they begin to function as company men they turn into inhuman monsters. Well, you do as you like," Mead concludes, "I won't sell. I'm going to the head office about this, and if need be, I'll go to Chicago and see the presi-

dent." Later, to his wife who also urges him to sell because
the company is so powerful that he cannot win: "Powerful
now, because it's fleecing us, but the little lamb is going to
bite back. That old story about the wolf in sheep's clothing is
passé. Now the sheep is getting a set of wolf's teeth, and he's
going to use them so that he can survive among the wolves!"
(pp. 88–89).

Lester Mead goes to Guatemala City, then on to Chicago,
but all he can elicit from the president is the statement that
the company is not a mutual-aid society. Shareholders are
interested in dividends; they do not care whether their investments foster ill will against Americans or not. Back in the
tropics, Mead calls a meeting of the Luceros and other planters
and proposes that they form a cooperative under his leadership.

The first thing to do is to begin practicing strict economy.
No more frittering away everything they earn on trifles and
luxuries. Their weakness had been that they lacked the means
to weather storms, and the company counts on this. Deliberately, it tries to enslave them by offering easy credit in
commissary stores, by encouraging everybody to buy and
buy and keep on buying. The cooperative will have to wage
an economic war. To solve the immediate problem, Mead
explains, he has brought back a truck; acting as partners they
will drive to neighboring towns, or even as far as the capital,
and sell their bananas to local markets. The last part of the
speech, if not the first, is something the planters can understand, and they accept the idea with relief.

The company is not treated directly in this novel. Its actions
can only be surmised through the reaction of the victims;
this device carries out the quality of depersonalization and
impassability that attaches to a huge corporation. One exception might be during the scene of Mead's interview with
the Green Pope, as the president is called. It is precisely there,
however, in the person of its chief representative, a monstrous
and evil puppet, alien to human life, that the company is
most forcefully dehumanized, thus rendering Surrealistically
Mead's impression of his antagonist.

The conflict between Mead and the company does not begin
until halfway through the book. Up to that point we witness a

leisurely presentation of setting: the heat of the Pacific coast, the greenness and profusion of the vegetation; the coast people, native and foreign; the mountain folk whose personality is shaped by their arid land. For the most part the characters are defined in their own idiom. As is his custom, Asturias sketches a vast number of people in few pages by lightning incursions into their consciousness or by briefly recording their personal view of life with his wonderful power of characterization.

The cooperative's adventures in resisting the time-tested maneuvers by which monopolies can eliminate competition are developed in three or four chapters. The partners are repeatedly saved by Mead's resourcefulness. They subsist by producing banana derivatives, by diversifying their crops and launching into any promising venture that presents itself. Indeed, Mead comes up with so many successful ideas for making money and they become so prosperous, that people begin to wonder. Old Lucero, now crippled with rheumatism, suspects Mead of having made a pact with the devil. Where does he get all the money? Trucks, trips to Chicago, land investments, purchase of equipment like the banana flour mill, and he a man who used to sell buttons from door to door! Do Lucero's sons know about it? the old man worries. Have they, too, sold their souls to the devil? Before he dies he intends to make them swear.... They're prosperous because they economize! argues Lucero's doctor. Still....

The most telling episode of the social theme concerns Mead's attempt to have two of his partners released from prison, where they were held illegally. By demonstrating that the laws of the country do not protect its citizens, these half-dozen pages attest the need and inevitability of revolution. The two men were arrested with a crowd of demonstrators and shipped to the capital in cattle cars. With spurious magnanimity the company pressed no charges against the "rebels," but its onesided report of the uprising was published in the daily papers and, through the magic power of the printed word, that report became incontrovertible fact; with the result that "public opinion" demanded that the prisoners be held and punished by forced labor. The papers refused to print Mead's statement rectifying the published report, telling him frankly that it would be against the interests of their major advertiser, the fruit company. Finally, it was only through bribery that he could obtain the release of his friends.

"Being an idealist, I suppose you disapprove of what we do," says a newspaper editor to Mead at one point.

"I'm a practical man; I don't disapprove of what you and your colleagues do. . . . But what is wrong in these countries, and it happens all the time, is that freedom is used to do away with freedom."

"Then you would recommend regulations?"

"I don't know what to say. As an American, I feel that freedom of the press is so precious that even manipulating public opinion in favor of special interests seems preferable to the least censorship or regulation" (pp. 134–35).

Matters extraneous to the social struggle are given as much emphasis as those which bear on it. For example, Asturias devotes a large section to the encounter of several men with their anima. Anima, as seen previously, is the name Jung has given to the feminine element of man's unconscious. It is not identical with the soul in the Christian sense. It is rather the personification of man's feminine nature. All that which a man feels as not belonging to himself, as nonmasculine, his moods, his irrationality, his capacity for infatuation, is constellated in the archetype of the anima and experienced as a being in the outside world. It can manifest itself in the shape of a goddess, a sprite, a siren, or it is projected upon one or more women. The anima is the archetype of the life principle.[2]

In *Viento fuerte* the anima does not appear in the shape of a goddess, as it did in *Hombres de maíz*, but as a personal, disruptive experience. Lino becomes enamored of a "woman of the sea," whom he perceives as an alluring mermaid with a provocative laugh and green flesh, colored by the green depths of the ocean. She is unbearably desirable and elusive. His friend Macario finds him down by the seashore, asleep or bewitched, with his arms around a tumbled banana tree; it is all Macario can do to keep him from following the mermaid into the ocean. But Macario is patient and understanding because he has been through this too. One night he split a banana tree with his machete and it fell forward on him, only as it fell it was transformed into a woman, a green entrancing female with a single leg; but after that night, no matter where he looked, he could never find her again. In both cases green, the life-color, appropriately symbolizes the anima's life-giving animating quality. The single leg or fishtail, like the serpent, is characteristic of the soul-image. The sea (water generally) is the most common symbol of the unconscious, as Jung has established, and the mermaid emerges from it, as the anima does from the unconscious. Well-known anima manifestations similar to Lino's and Macario's are the negative figures of Circe, nixies, Lilith, and the Lorelei.

When Lino loses the sense of his sea-woman's magic presence, he falls back on the bottle and drags around looking for her, equally unmindful of his wife and mother's tears as of his father's outrage. The family goes to Mead: perhaps if he spoke to Lino...? Mead hears them glumly but makes no move. "Tell them to leave Lino alone," he mutters later to his wife; he has just gotten over his own "mermaid," a Spanish dancer who drove him to the extremes of desire and anger simultaneously by her flippant chatter about his flour mill (p. 162). He took his revenge on her by buying her, then stamping out of her room without touching her. This is a typical anima-possession in a modern man, whose rationalized world, emptied of symbols, compels him to project the contents of his unconscious on human personalities. A dancing girl is a most suitable recipient.[3]

During a party at the Meads, Leland brings up the question of whether mermaids really exist, and a Mr. O'Briend (*sic*) tells of one he saw in a tropical sea. Although it was night and she did not show herself distinctly, he clearly recognized her, just as in dreams one knows who people are without having seen them before. The fugitive passage of the mermaid through the water drew him with such sweet force that much later, when he was aroused from his ecstasy, he found himself on the verge of falling overboard. O'Briend's experience illustrates the treacherous pull of the unconscious: recognition is a characteristic of these anima encounters: a man knows at once that this is "she"

There is a fifth man in the novel who says his "mermaid" is a bottle of Chianti, for the sake of which he has sold himself to the company. Drunkenness that is no longer a temporary crisis indicates regression into the unconscious with a corresponding disintegration of the personality. Where Macario, Mead, and O'Briend have recovered from their bewitchment, the Italian has not, and Lino's case is still undecided.

Of the five men negatively assailed by their anima, only Mead withstood its regressive pull, when by conscious exertion he turned his back on the dancer and left her. Like the classic example of Ulysses, he was able to face and conquer the danger of his Circe. As for Lino, his vitality is so reduced by malarial fevers from sleeping in the damp banana groves that he is moved to look for Rito Perraj, the local shaman. Rito is a widely revered hermit and wonder-worker. As happens with most seers, magicians, and witch doctors, many of the qualities attributed to Rito are projections of a psychic nature. On the level of Maya theology, the threefold aspect of his personality, whereby he is at once Grandfather, Father, and Grandson, identifies him with the trinitarian manifestation of the Maya sun god; in his three persons Rito, like the sun, incarnates past, present, and future, which expresses the wisdom, power, and continued vitality of that supreme deity.[4] It is the function of a mana personality (i.e., endowed with extraordinary powers) to be the object of such projections.

On a personal level, the shaman embodies the archetype of the wise old man for Lino at this moment. This archetype derives from a stage in human development when man did not consciously think, but perceived en bloc, and considered his perceptions or what one might call, unconscious thoughts, to be revelations reaching him from an outside source. This source, which assumes such varied forms as oracles, fairy godmothers, helpful animals, prophets, is what Jung calls the archetype of the wise old man; he has shown that what seems to come from on high is in reality the voice of the unconscious.[5]

In his condition Lino has no stamina for extricating himself from the impasse to which his unconscious has led him; reflection, determination, and good advice are in order at this juncture, which are what the shaman will provide. Because

he is a source of illumination, the wise old man is often identified with the sun, as Rito was; still oftener he asks questions
which have the effect of eliciting reflection. Rito does likewise:
Who is Lino? His family? His friends? Occupation? When did
time begin to count for him? As Lino turns over these questions
in his mind, his consciousness begins to function again, ever so
weakly. The first thing he knows he finds himself back home
with a laxative to take, certain seeds to chew and, within two
weeks' time, back to normal. What, in effect, has the wise
old shaman done other than by his mere presence to draw out
the psychic energy which was already striving within Lino for
his rehabilitation? It was an inner urgency of the patient that
sent him to Rito Peraj in the first place.[6]

Toward the end of *Viento fuerte* Mead and his wife fly to
New York where a surprise awaits her: she finds out that her
husband is the largest stockholder of the banana company
and that he has been living incognito in the tropics to observe
its methods of operation for a group of other well-meaning
investors. (One of Mead's guiding maxims is that a millionaire
is a man who is rich enough to afford the luxury of not being a
scoundrel.) Now he has come back to report on his findings.
His address, according to Asturias, is based on an actual report
made by two American journalists.[7] The point Mead stresses,
and which is variously stated throughout this and the next
book, is that it would not cost the company a penny in profits
to contribute to the well-being of the native peoples, to respect
the laws of the land, eliminate bribery, and to renounce the
high-handed methods which demolish the prestige of the
United States: "We are not hated because we are Americans,
but because we are bad Americans. If the world situation
were ever to turn against us, the hatred of thousands would
accompany us, a hatred we have earned by our voracity,
bringing ruin to local economies. Nor do the benefits of civilization that we pride ourselves in having introduced to those
regions compensate for our ruthlessness. How can we boast
of saving a man from malaria if we cause him to drink himself
to death out of despair?" (pp. 180–81).

Before leaving New York, Mead sees his lawyers about a
new will bequeathing his entire fortune to his wife or in her

default to the cooperative. He also obtains a loan to finance the development of banana derivatives. Some time after the Meads have returned to the tropics, the area is devastated by a windstorm or, in planters' parlance, a blowdown, the "strong wind" of the title. It roots up trees and tears down buildings, but a prophecy warns that the hurricane is only the forerunner of a greater storm that the workers will unleash some day against the fruit company.

In primitive philosophy nothing ever happens by chance. The cause of the blowdown is popularly held to have been the vengeance of a native planter. This man had been ruined by the company, and in order to get even, he struck a bargain with Rito Perraj whereby in exchange for his life the shaman would provoke a storm strong enough to sweep the company and its plantations into the sea. We follow the sorcerer as he carries out his black magic with the planter's head, recites incantations, and calls upon the gods Huracán (Hurricane) and Cabracán (Earthquake) to send the storm. When the wind reaches its peak he goes back to the cemetery with the skull and buries it in its proper grave. During this storm, Leland and Lester Mead are killed and the novel closes as a train carries their bodies away through the flattened banana plantations to some foreigners' cemetery, whereas their rightful place was there in the little tropical town they loved.

Asturias has been criticized for admitting folklore and magical elements into his novels of social reality. It is alleged that by so doing he dilutes the impact of their message. But folklore and magic, gods and myths, are part of Guatemalan reality, he answers. "My novels are realistic precisely because they do include these aspects; because the witch doctor or the God Huracán assumes an overwhelming reality for the people of our country, because the storm which destroys the banana plantation may be very real, but for our Indians it also assumes magical proportions. This mentality molds the people's spirit and thinking in a very profound way. So, too, in 'Strong Wind' social reality is combined with an element of magic."[8]

The same may be said of the psychological experiences undergone by various Asturias characters: the experiences are a part of reality, in Guatemala as in any corner of the world, although all men are not equally aware of them. The sudden infatuation of a happily married, middle-aged businessman with a dancing girl glimpsed in a customs office is of the same nature and stems from the same source as an Indian's vision of Huracán and Cabracán: both are spontaneous manifestations of the unconscious.

The subsequent books of the trilogy can be read independently, but the specific virtue of *Viento fuerte* is that it establishes the nature and mentality of the Guatemalan worker and his problematic relationship with the foreign presence he depends upon. It illustrates the growing social awareness learned from experience by the new generations in contrast with the individualism of early laborers like Adelaido Lucero, who worked on the principle "each man for himself." It marks the people's growing disillusionment with the fruit company as the momentum of uncurbed profit making begins to be felt. Although the novel has no precise message, the reader can infer from the example of Mead's cooperative that any local resistance by the natives to the power of the trust is out of the question. Only money, knowledge, and business skill equal to the company's, such as Mead had, could pretend to match wits with it; therefore, Lester Mead's efforts brought no practical solution to the workers' problems. In short, *Viento fuerte* defines the setting and circumstances of a segment of Guatemala which on the one hand serves Asturias' general aim of depicting the reality of Latin America, and on the other hand, heralds the social revolution and promise of reformation with which the trilogy is meant to close.

In writing about the social novels of Asturias, the tendency has been to furnish a running account of actual events or conditions which seem to parallel certain situations in the plot. In point of fact, there have been boundary disputes where colonial documents were used; there have been sudden reductions of price from sixty to twenty-four cents a stem; private growers have been reduced to bankruptcy by United Fruit Company policy; the press has been controlled and cooperative ventures frustrated; strikes have occurred simultaneously with revolutions.

Nearly all the outrages that plague the characters of Asturias' trilogy may be found in *The Banana Empire: A Case*

Study in Economic Imperialism, reporting on the activities of the United Fruit Company throughout its Central and South American holdings. A brief glance through the 390 pages of this study is sufficient to recognize it as the sourcebook for many episodes in the trilogy, as Asturias stated in an interview.[9] The only liberty Asturias took in elaborating this material for his novel was to transfer it all to Guatemala, whereas in some cases the original event may have occurred in another of the republics that were hosts to the United Fruit Company.

CHAPTER 7

El Papa Verde

I *Plot Summary*

IN *El papa verde* (The Green Pope, 1954), Asturias takes us back again to the early days of the fruit company's foundation, but this time on the Atlantic coast. Nothing grandiose or epic here. The area in question is inland and upstream from the port, and it has long been settled and under cultivation. Small farmers bring their produce to the docks and sell it to the company-owned mailboat. The stateside demand for bananas being greater than the local people can or care to supply, the company has decided to establish a more dependable and productive source of bananas by buying up the best land and planting their own. The man contracted to carry out this project, Geo Maker Thompson, is a young American familiar with the area for having plied the Caribbean coastal waters in his own cargo steamship for some years. The chance encounter of a buyer for his broken-down freighter leads him from shipping to planting, or in the author's terms, transforms him from a pirate of the high seas into an inland pirate, navigating on a sea of human sweat. Indeed, this twenty-five-year-old blond, tall, athletic, and ambitious, pictures himself as a modern Sir Francis Drake, and for his new task he has appropriated the title of Green Pope (el Papa Verde).[1] His rise to power as the eventual president of the fruit company is the core of this novel. It is the closest Asturias has come to writing an outright character study: *El Señor Presidente* is such a study (of Miguel Cara de Angel) but handled so abstrusely as to pass unnoticed by many readers.

In order to establish the company on the Atlantic coast, GMT travels up the valley of the Motagua River offering to buy all the productive lands. High prices are offered, and farmers who refuse to sell are warned that they will be evicted anyway for impeding the progress and development of the nation. In this matter GMT has secured the support of army and government officials through bribery. The farmers may stay on and work for the company, but in order to gather them together where he can control them, GMT builds new barracks and housing for them around his headquarters. Then he sets fire to the native shacks under pretext of plague and disease prevention.

He is largely successful in his general plan of bringing the fertile region under his management; instead of buying the lands, however, he has to usurp them, because most of the natives refuse to sell. Their opposition comes from their deep attachment to the soil. To their way of thinking, their parcel of land, no matter how unproductive, is more precious than any amount of money. It simply has no price. There is a mystique attached to the possession of land; it is what gives a man freedom and dignity. Land has more meaning than life and ultimately more meaning than the individual himself. "To sell your land when you don't have to is like selling Our Lord," says one of the characters.[2]

GMT's servant, Chipo Chipó, an Indian who shares these feelings, precedes his employer among the scattered homes to warn the people not to sell; he explains that if they are evicted, the government will some day restitute the lands to them as long as they do not relinquish their title.

Another source of opposition to GMT comes from his own fiancée. He fell in love with Mayarí, a golden-skinned beauty, in the port town just as he was starting on his venture. From the beginning she knew his ideas on domineering the peasants by sheer force, but when she began to see his words being put into action, she became horrified at what he was doing to her people. She disappears from her home and joins Chipo Chipó in his self-imposed mission. Not knowing about GMT's bribery (and the venality of her country's officials) she urges the small landowners to appeal to the central government for help. Mayarí is an educated middle-class girl, but she is nonetheless imbued with the traditions and myths of the Indians of Guatemala. After discharging what she considers to be her social duty toward her people, she withdraws to attend her own destiny. On the night of the brightest full moon of the year she dons her satin wedding gown and a crown of tiny white shells (universal fertility symbols), as she prepares to become the bride of the River Motagua. Sitting in Chipo Chipó's *piragua*, she rides down the current under the bright tropical moon through lines of other flower-decked boats that have come to greet her. Then, in a secret place, the mystical marriage takes place. While she was in no way constrained to this form of death but stepped freely and eagerly into the embrace of her spouse (there are other indications of her suicidal tendency), the local Indians, particularly the shaman, look upon her action as a sacrifice. Some offer this sacrifice to the gods amid clouds of *pom* incense to obtain deliverance from their abysmal distress; others, with limited awareness of social happenings, even those that affect them, are only conscious of the fertility aspect of this particular night.

When there is still hope of finding Mayarí, GMT gets drunk in the company of some friends. Through a misunderstanding he thinks one of them is telling him to forget her. "No! No!" he shouts. "Shut up! Shut up!, and he charges off to the seashore, along the half-submerged islands where he and the girl had gone wading together. He shouts her name, promising to give up the scheme she hated and to go back to pearl fishing if only she will come back to him. "Mayaríííí! Come back! The Green Pope is finished! I'm going back to sea! I'm giving up the plantations! Come back now!" (p. 71).

The peculiarity of GMT's character is that the evil in him is not there by nature but by design, because he has so willed it, so that when he is drunk and his controls are down it is not further depravity that is revealed, as with ordinary men, but a repressed propensity for self-sacrifice and love. This is the surprising irony that captures the reader's sympathy for GMT, or at any rate his interest. Furthermore, as in the case of *El Señor Presidente*'s Cara de Angel, it establishes the ambiguity of GMT's character and prepares for the unexpected reversal that is to disrupt his life when his conscience will step in and check the impetus of his ambition.

With the return of consciousness, GMT regains control of his better nature and soon succeeds in establishing the plantations; he clears the area of its former inhabitants by means of fire and gun and puts it rapidly under production. Like the conquistadors of old, who destroyed the Indians' idols and art work in the name of religion, GMT burns the belongings of their descendants in the name of sanitation, and the natives are left with the choice of either coming to live in his barracks and working for him or moving away. The younger ones fall in with the first proposition, whereas most of the older people leave or commit suicide.

In reality, the little company town, offices, hospital, housing, hotel, which GMT is supposed to have founded, and his plantations, refer in a general way to the United Fruit holdings near Puerto Barrios, Guatemala, along the southern edge of which, according to guidebooks, the railroad runs twenty-three miles, from Bananera, the headquarters, to Quiriguá, near the famous Maya ruins.

The text skips ten years and now the portraits of three women stand on GMT's desk: Mayarí, his love; Doña Flora, his wife, and Aurelia, his daughter. Doña Flora was the mother of Mayarí, an energetic businesswoman who helped him clear the Motagua Valley of its inhabitants. We learn that GMT married her after Mayarí's disappearance and that she died in childbirth. Aurelia, their daughter and Mayarí's little sister, is away at school in British Honduras.

A visitor from the United States, Charles Peifer is inspecting the plantations in a railcar. He tells GMT, his guide, that he has been talking with the workers and has learned that the company has no title to the plantations, no legal right to operate them, and that it is only by bribing the central government that it manages to remain in the country at all. He has gathered careful documentation on this matter, he says, and as soon as he gets back to the United States he will make a report to the proper authorities. Guessing that the visitor is really Richard Wotton, one of the company's critics, traveling in disguise to collect prejudicial data on its operational tactics, GMT decides at once to take action. As the tour by railcar continues, he drives fast along a dangerous curve, leaps out of the car as it derails into a ravine, and ships the remains of Charles Peifer back to the United States in a box.

Another time lapse and GMT is back in the port town where he first met Mayarí. He has come to meet his daughter Aurelia who has finished her schooling and is returning after many years' absence. He is eager to see if she will look like her sister Mayarí, and as he waits for the ship he imagines that he is the one who is returning from the high seas, while Mayarí stands on the dock watching for him.

Aurelia is not like Mayarí, and she notices her father's disappointment. She develops into an attractive girl, however, and meets Ray Salcedo, an archeologist who is studying the Quiriguá ruins. While her father is in Chicago on business, she yields to the young man. She does it out of a sense of revenge, to make up for the time when her appearance had been so disappointing to her father. Revenge against whom? She knows not, but in the moment of surrender to the archeologist she throws back her head like the sacrificial victim of an Indian rite, as if her breast were to be pierced with an obsidian knife and her heart lifted out like a fluttering firebird. Later, when the young man has departed for some other archeological site, she remembers the ballad he sang for her about Tam Lin, a legendary character who was in love with a fairy. In the ballad, Tam Lin tells the fairy that he will be changed into a serpent, an alligator, and other strange forms, but that she must hold him tightly in her arms and cover him with her green cloak, because he is the father of her child. "The father of your child," she repeats musingly (p. 105). Although she never did anything to find him again, such was Ray Salcedo to be: the father of her child. The child will be called Boby (*sic*) Thompson.

GMT was in Chicago, his home town, to promote an old scheme of his for annexing Guatemala to the United States. At company headquarters he explains his idea to a United States senator. By enumerating the many concessions already granted the company by complaisant dictators and the unlawful power the company is allowed to exercise by corrupt officials, he convinces the senator that the little country could be taken over peaceably. GMT, the Banana King, as Chicago designates its native son, has his eye on the governorship of the annexed territory. His fame and success also put him in the position where he may be elected the next president of the fruit company.

The senator goes to Washington to confer with the State Department, and GMT to meet his daughter and hear about her pregnancy. In this interim a bombshell explodes in the form of a documented report on the abuses of the company in its Central American operations, presented to the Washington government. The annexation scheme is off. The author of the report is Richard Wotton, the old enemy. "That is impossible," objects GMT, "Richard Wotton died years ago in an accident while he was visiting the plantations." ("I should know," he adds mentally, "I killed him".) "No, that was Charles Peifer," says the president of the fruit company; "he left a widow and three children, and they're all going to vote for you at the next stockholders' meeting. Richard Wotton is not dead, or if he was he's come back to life again! He was down your way just recently posing as an archeologist. Now the first thing we must do is to bury this report under an avalanche of publicity. The company's largess must be extolled, our hospitals, our commissary stores; schools must be built; the enthusiasm of the workers, jobs, high salaries. Lots of pictures a minimum of text!" (pp. 128–29).

But GMT is not listening. His mind is on Charles Peifer. He walks out into the streets of Chicago where hour after hour he paces the length and breadth of the city. Not to be able to recall Peifer from death. A wife and children who will vote for him. He must withdraw his candidacy. If he could only recall Peifer to life. Recall from life the creature in Aurelia's womb, Richard Wotton's son. To have reached the heights of power and wealth and to be unable to buy back the body of Charles Peifer. The cries "Banana King! Green Pope!" echo in his ears. Who tricked him? Not Richard Wotton, who never knew about Charles Peifer or his accident, who could not have known about the annexation project. Fate. Irremediable fate. The perfect crime committed against the wrong man! And then the final enigma: Aurelia's pregnancy. Endlessly, like the tune in a music box, the mystery hammers in GMT's brain, as the voices of newboys fill the night: "The Green Pope withdraws to private life! Refuses the presidency of the fruit company!" (p. 131).

So ends Part I, comprising eight chapters out of the total seventeen. The following six have little to do with GMT, and he only begins to take an active role again in the remaining three. This is a serious gap if the novel is to be considered his story, as the title suggests. If, however, the author's aim is to fill in another panel in his great mural of Guatemala, as is likely, the apparent interruption is no such thing at all but constitutes instead an organic fragment of his project.

Part II begins ten to twelve years after GMT's retirement, judging from the age of his grandson, Boby Thompson, to whose gang or baseball team many pages are devoted, and one year after the death of the Meads. The newspapers are full of the arrival in Guatemala of two lawyers from New York on their way to the Pacific coast to read the last will and testament of Lester Mead. The heirs of his great fortune are the seven members of his cooperative. Asturias takes full advantage of the excitement by dramatizing at length the reaction of these men and of their wives, of various towns-people, company officials, and even strangers in distant parts of the country who read about it in the newspapers; in this way he also provides a synopsis of the main features of *Viento fuerte* and further clarification on that plot.

The Luceros throw a party to which everyone is invited, including the commander of the troops stationed in town to protect the company and its hierarchy. Toward the end of the fiesta this officer makes a speech to announce that soldiers have been stationed around the homes of each of the new millionaires in order to protect them from the populace, from beggars, swindlers, and all similar annoyances. In response, Lino Lucero rises and in the name of the cooperative refuses the offered protection. He and his associates, he says, have nothing to fear from the populace, being themselves men of the populace. They have no intention of becoming enemies of the workers by reason of their inheritance, nor of going over to the side of those who exploit them. The capital they have received in trust from the founder of their cooperative will be used to continue his ideals. As for handouts, he lets it be known that no money will be distributed in charities because the members of the cooperative learned from Lester

Mead and Leland Foster never to degrade a man or to wound his dignity by giving him alms, but instead to provide him with the opportunity for self-help.

Whereupon another member of the cooperative jumps up to dissociate himself from Lino's declaration and to assert that he does require the protection of the guard until such time as he and his family can depart for the United States. As a result, the cooperative falls apart. Four of the partners leave the coast, move into higher social circles, and disappear from the novels. The three Lucero brothers remain in the old homestead to carry out the work of Lester Mead, and although they too inevitably move into higher circles, they remain active in the social life of the little company town.

A dispute arises between the Guatemala branch of the fruit company and the Honduras division over a matter of boundaries which threatens to involve the nation in a war with its neighbor. This is where GMT swings back into action. He is now described as *old* Maker Thompson, aged perhaps by experience rather than years. His long retirement, or more exactly, the checkmate inflicted upon him by destiny and his conscience, have mellowed him. He befriends Lino Lucero toward whom he feels an unexplained sympathy, and he confides to him, as he watches Boby go off to play with Lino's son, that life would have little meaning without this grandson of his: two human symptoms in a man who was once a nearly inhuman dynamo.

He also expounds to Lucero, by means of a metaphor, what was the essential fallacy of Lester Mead's position, and therefore that of the Luceros': wealth is, unfortunately, a hank of greedy ambitions, a nauseating snarl from which a strand may be isolated just as with a comb one separates a lock from a mop of hair. Superficially, the lock can be set aside, but underneath it remains joined to the scalp, drawing upon whatever there may be under its roots good or bad which feeds the rest of the hair. "You and your brothers have generously set aside the shares which you own in the fruit company in order to follow in the steps of Lester Mead, but only apparently so, because underneath, at bottom, your shares are still feeding upon that which sustains all the other shares"

(p. 256). Here, once more, and this time unequivocally, the Mead ideology is exploded, because in spite of its apparent nobility it is built upon gross self-deception. The humbling of the great corporation will be the work of a man whose mind is undivided and who can consecrate the entire thrust of his energies to the task.

It is not clear whether Lino Lucero ever grasps the incongruity of his posture but be it from apathy, greed, or incompetence, his good intentions do in fact become increasingly ineffectual, and his energies expend themselves in words. Within a decade or less, by the time of the revolution which closes the third book of the trilogy, he and his brothers have passed over to the side of the fruit company. Due to unfounded fear of the strikers, they ask for the police protection against the workers which they had so proudly rejected, thus identifying with the "enemy". The Luceros' stand of giving no alms degenerates into their refusing any help whatsoever to the people, arguing that the latter are fighting for their bellies, not for ideals as had the cooperative.

After reminding Lucero how much the latter is part of the company he professes to fight, GMT asks him if he would consider supporting his own candidacy for president at the next stockholders' meeting: if he is elected, he explains, he will be able to prevent the border war and at the same time to insure the preponderance of the Guatemala division over the Honduras district. This will be beneficial both to Lucero's country and to the value of the Luceros' stocks. From an attitude of mistrust toward the Green Pope, Lino swings around and becomes his enthusiastic supporter; the two youngsters, Boby and the Lucero boy, become inseparable.

The border controversy is submitted to Washington for arbitration; the prevailing opinion is that Honduras will win the dispute; a document from colonial times turns up which seems to settle the matter. Everyone who has securities in the Guatemala division wants to sell or exchange them for Honduras stock. The only person who is buying Guatemala stock is GMT. Sitting in a Chicago hotel room with the old cry "Green Pope! Banana King!" ringing again in his ears, he purchases all the shares the others are unloading, encouraging

them to sell, although in the case of the Lucero brothers he
refuses to touch their holdings. His friends ask him and ask
each other why he is ruining himself this way. Is he determined
to go down with his ship like the old mariner that he is? Or
is it pride that keeps him from admitting his company's defeat?
He takes Aurelia aside, makes her sit at his feet like a child,
and tells her a story about men who can turn themselves into
wolves by the light of the moon, and who in the shape of wolves,
commit all sorts of atrocities. (Werewolves in Spanish are
lobisones.) Only a superstition. Not the sort of thing that
can happen. And yet it does. It happens not only in remote,
backward places, but in Washington itself, in the Capitol.
There, men can be found who, by the light of gold pieces,
can be turned into lobbyists. (*Lobisones* and *lobbystas* sound
alike, and in the text the word play which relates the werewolves to the lobbyists is quite plain.)

Not until after Aurelia has repeated this story to someone
else does the meaning of it dawn upon her. She runs to the
telephone, calls her broker and orders him to switch all her
holdings back to Guatemala division stocks: thus she saves
herself from ruin. The Luceros were also saved by the old
man's refusal to buy their securities, because when word came
through from Washington, the arbiters had pronounced in
favor of Guatemala. *El papa verde* closes as GMT, accompanied
by his daughter and surrounded by his friends and enemies,
marches down the hall with his heavy planter's tread to take
over the presidency of the company of which he is now the
major stockholder.

His part in the third book will be very small: he is mostly
seen at a distance and from the point of view of the strike
leaders, as he deals unsympathetically with their demands
from his deathbed a few years later. He dies of throat cancer,
with Aurelia at his side, and thinking of Boby his grandson.
Some critics in writing of this astute entrepreneur have said
that solitude marked his life and was his punishment, but there
is no evidence for this puritanical interpretation. While he
often did think of Mayarí, it is not indicated that he minded
his solitude, nor that he yearned for companionship; he died
in a happy mood just after a hallucination in which Boby had

visited him, and Aurelia could not bring herself to tell him that the boy had been shot to death. Yet, if life can ever be thought to bring retribution to the wrongdoer, it seems more likely that GMT's punishment came not from loneliness but from his fate, from that chance combination of circumstances which, at the moment of triumph, caused his conscience to throw into reverse gear the momentum of his ambition. After that setback he was never quite the same man again; witness his handling of Lino Lucero, a potential threat to the company, as compared to his earlier handling of the Peifer-Wotton threat or of any other obstacle to the company's prodigious growth.

Regarding the factual basis for *El papa verde*, I would only note that *The Banana Empire*, mentioned at the end of the previous chapter, tells of a certain Mr. Zemurry, a New Orleans banana jobber, who became the largest stockholder in the United Fruit Company, ousted the president, and seized control of the corporation. Although the circumstances of this man's rise to power are entirely different from GMT's career, they certainly may have sparked the idea for it.

II *Mythical Structure*

It is interesting to notice that in broad outline Geo Maker Thompson and his family represent some of the major Maya gods. It is a pity that these gods are not familiar to us because their myths are as lovely as any from the old world, and they have exactly the same meaning.

GMT's uncommon name, Geo, means earth. Geo Maker, as Aurelia insisted on calling her father, Earth Maker, suggests that he is connected with the creator gods, who in Maya Quiché theology are also called Makers, inasmuch as their creation was not *ex nihilo*. Before anything was made, the *Popol Vuh* explains, when there was only the sky and the sea, the Creators and the Makers lived in the water, concealed by green feathers. Their generic name was *Gucumatz*, which means quetzal/snake, or commonly Feathered Serpent. These green feathers of the quetzal were the insignia of the gods and of Indian nobility. GMT's title, Papa Verde, which can mean Green Father, relates him to Gucumatz; and just as

Gucumatz is connected with the sea, GMT had been a pirate and came out of the sea (he is called amphibious). He may even be said to have been a "maker" of Guatemalan geography inasmuch as whole towns were wiped out to make way for the huge, fertile plantations.

Gucumatz, an avatar of the sun, was sustained by blood, preferably human. Of GMT it can be said that, in addition to all those who were destroyed by his ambition, the three women of his life were sacrificed to him: Mayarí, obviously so; Aurelia, figuratively, because she identified her relations with Ray Salcedo with having her heart cut out, and surrendered to him thinking of her father; finally, Doña Flora, the girls' mother, died in childbirth, and to the Indians of Central America this was a form of sacrifice comparable to the death of a warrior. GMT used to say ironically that his wife had "died in action." On an earlier occasion GMT noticed that Flora, with her hooked nose and sloping shoulders, resembled the sacred Maya tapir. This animal was an emblem of the Great Mother Xmucané, the feminine counterpart of Gucumatz, as Doña Flora is the counterpart of GMT.

Furthermore, GMT, whose stature made him seem gigantic to Indian laborers, is assimilated to Huracán, the Giant of the Wind, another major deity. In the novel, a fanciful story circulated about GMT. It was said that one night a thunderbolt had struck him and reduced him to ashes; then for an instant he became a streak of lightning, and in that instant everything he touched was turned into gold; the vibration of the thunder multiplied his hands so that he was able to reach out and touch all the lands that today are producing millions of stems of green gold, the favorite bananas of the western hemisphere; and finally, from a streak of lightning he was transformed into what he truly was, the Green Pope. On the image level this is a beautiful, extended metaphor, a poetic fable summing up GMT's career. On the mythic level it identifies him with Huracán, because during the rainy season this god took over the function of storm god, and as such he had three manifestations: Thunder, Lightning, and Thunderbolt. (In lightning, the zigzag serpent seen in the sky was distinguished from

the light which illuminates the countryside, and called respectively *rayo* and *relámpago*.)

Regarding Aurelia and Richard Wotton, alias Ray Salcedo,
it appears that she is Xquic, and that he fills the part of Hun-
Hunahpú, the Quiché agrarian god who with his twin went to
the underworld, lost the ritual ball game, died by decapitation,
and was reborn in his son Hunahpú (see note 3, Chapter 3
above). His head was hung on a calabash tree, but with his
spittle he impregnated Xquic; the head symbolizes the corn
seed that produces the new corn plant. As a result of her
inexplicable pregnancy, it was ordered that the young girl
Xquic should have her heart torn out (we already know how
Aurelia imagined her heart was being removed); but Xquic
substituted the red sap of a resinous tree for her heart and
lived to bear her son.

Hun-Hunahpú as fertility god was really an aspect of the
sun; in practice he was often called *el Rey* (the King). The
equivalence between Rey and Ray is pointed out in the novel.
Wotton's real name, Richard, means *strong king*. Wotton
probably stands for Votán, a Maya variant of the Hunahpú
family of culture gods. Richard Wotton "died," so far as
GMT was concerned, and when his damaging report on the
fruit company appeared, he "came back to life." This was
mockingly said to GMT, who kept insisting that Wotton was
dead. The animal symbols of Hun-Hunahpú were the serpent,
the alligator or any such aquatic monster, because being a
fertility god he was connected with the rainy season and with
water. In the ballad Ray sang to Aurelia, where Tam Lin
obviously referred to himself, he predicted he would be transformed variously into a serpent, an alligator, and a deer (another creature of the Quiché sun cult), but that she must
cover him with her green mantle, for he was the father of her
child. The green mantle is the fertile surface of the earth,
and Aurelia is the earth, just as Xquic and all Great Mothers
are. Tam Lin/Ray is the grain of corn in her bosom, as is
Hun-Hunahpú, and the child is the young corn plant, or Boby.
Interwoven through the pages that describe Ray and Aurelia's
affair are the thoughts of Juambo, a mulatto servant who

observed them. He hums a waltz about the good French King
(*el Rey*) who lost his crown and his head: this recalls that
Hun-Hunahpú lost his head on the ball court; Ray Salcedo
played tennis. In this context, Juambo probably represents
the Lords of Death, Hun-Hunahpú's enemies, usually shown
with dark face paint in Maya art.

Hunahpú, the young corn and sun god, was a great ball
player like his father and uncle, the twins; he was also a skillful
hunter, striking his prey with pellets from his blowgun. Like
him, Boby Thompson was an assiduous ballplayer (baseball
in this case). He was captain of his team, both by virtue of
his natural leadership and because of his admirable collection
of gloves, bats, and other baseball gear. In the sacred ball
game of the Maya gods, the playing gear was the insignia of
the solar god, the ball in particular, for it represented the sun
as it flew through the skies. Boby was a reddish blond, which
is characteristic of corn gods (with reference to corn silk) and
of the sun; often his hair is described as flamelike or shiny.
His name, Robert, means bright, gleaming. Thomas means
twin, therefore Thompson means son of the twin; Hunahpú
was the son of a twin.

In the third book of the trilogy Boby is fifteen or sixteen
and still leads a gang, but a mischievous one now. As a consequence of pitching practice no doubt, his impulse is always to
throw, and on various occasions he imitates Hunahpú, pelting
things and people with whatever comes to hand. At about
this time in the novel, Juambo, the old mulatto servant of
the Thompsons, becomes obsessed with the idea of making
reparation to his father for past wrongs. He digs up his father's
bones, talks to them, and rearranges them in the grave. In
the course of one of his pranks, Boby surprises Juambo in
the cemetery one night and in horror tries to drag the old
fellow away. This recalls an incident in *Popol Vuh* where
Hunahpú, having vanquished the underworld, digs up the
remains of his father and uncle in the ball court and addresses
them, declaring that their bones shall not be lost nor their
names forgotten; then he reburies them in a proper manner.

Boby died shortly after the cemetery incident, shot by a
woman who mistook him for Juambo. He lay on the road,

his flaming hair surmounting his face like smoke, eyes downcast, mouth half open—a description that recalls the Copán statue of the handsome young sun god whose tousled hair represents sunrays. Boby's remains were flown to Chicago where his hysterical mother, Aurelia, conceives the notion that he must have a tomb in the sky. A plane containing his body is kept aloft for weeks, flying around and around, refueled by another plane, until it falls into the sea—or so she is told. This is akin to the myth of Hunahpú who, having finished his tasks, rose into the heavens and became the sun. The idea of Boby's body falling into the sea corresponds to the setting of the sun.

The three gods whom GMT, Wotton, and Boby impersonate are really alter egos of one and the same god, the sun: the elder as the great father and creator (Papa Verde), the second as the cause and promoter of growth, and the younger, the morning sun, as the divine corn plant. Xmucané and Xquic whom Doña Flora and Aurelia impersonate, are the old moon and the full moon respectively. Mayarí, Aurelia's sister, is just a variant of Xquic, probably Xtabay, the goddess of suicide. The bewitching Xtabay lured men to their death, just as one night Mayarí nearly lured GMT out into the sea.

CHAPTER 8

Los ojos de los enterrados

THE title of *Los ojos de los enterrados*, 1960 (The Eyes of the Buried) is derived from a saying according to which anyone who has suffered injustice and dies without redress, lies in his grave with his eyes open until he is avenged. In this context the title refers to the successful revolution at the end of the book which brings down simultaneously both the dictator and the fruit company and avenges all the victims of exploitation, the living and the dead. A descriptive subtitle might have been "The Birth of a Nation," especially in the novel's original version; Asturias has said that he had just finished writing it in 1954 when the democratically elected government of Guatemala was toppled. He left the book alone for a long time, but in 1959 he decided he would have to adjust his text to the sad shape of history and began to revise it. Apparently he dropped one whole chapter (Chapter 27 is missing) and reworked the novel so as to have it end on a note of hope rather than one of triumph as before. One suspects that the insertions are those passages which appear toward the end, whose strident, angry tones are so unlike any of the author's earlier writings, but which do resemble the spirit of *Week-end en Guatemala*, short stories written immediately after the 1954 debacle.

Los ojos is the longest novel by Asturias, five hundred pages. Except for a hundred-page flashback, the action takes place during the last few weeks of preparation for the strike. The protagonist is Octavio Sansur, an orphan brought up in the slums of Guatemala by a lady fortune teller. He was too smart to be wasted on public schools, she would say, and she could not afford to send him to a private one, so she apprenticed him to a barber in whose shop he would meet the best people. One of the barbers taught him to read and from then on he educated himself; the French Revolution enthralled him, particularly the ideas of Jean Paul Marat. His first juvenile gesture of rebellion consisted in freeing the birds of a pet shop while shouting the *Marseillaise* and earned him a police record. He fled to Panama where he adopted the pseudonym Juan Pablo Mondragón, Juan Pablo after Marat, and Mondragón after the barber who taught him his letters.

Ten or fifteen years later found him back in Guatemala, conspiring against the life of the president. His own idea was to incite an uprising among the people in order to overthrow the government from the bottom up; but the other members of the conspiracy, being of the middle class, were aware that in such an uprising their own interests would be endangered. Sansur had to settle for an assassination. Being without family ties or personal ambitions, he volunteered for the most dangerous assignment. The conspiracy was discovered, and it was only through mere chance that he was not caught.

Two old Indians hide him and help him escape through caves and underground passages known only to themselves, ancient lava beds leading clear through the volcanoes to the south coast. There he disappears into the "great human swamp" of unskilled laborers toiling in the banana plantations. Wanted dead or alive, he can pass unnoticed thanks to certain fungi that temporarily disfigure his features, another secret learned from his Indian saviors.

While hauling stems from the banana groves to the freight trains, Sansur begins to realize that he has stumbled onto the tap root that sustains the dictatorship—the fruit company. It becomes clear to him that to try to overthrow the one and not the other is futile. The twin powers are interdependent, for as the cloud carries the storm within its bosom, so does the trust carry the dictatorship. They must be approached and brought down together. An assignment of this nature is not one that could be entrusted to a clique of conspirators like those Sansur has known previously; insurrections by such groups amount to little more than a palace mutiny. Now more than ever Sansur knows that he must follow his own instinct: the struggle is to be won only by the combined efforts of the people themselves.

Without forsaking his work among the fruit haulers, Sansur first sets himself to organizing a peasant uprising; but later the idea of a general strike occurs to him. He sees it as a non-violent revolution that will take the government by surprise; fully prepared for any kind of violence, the authorities would be helpless against the inaction of a general strike. Furthermore, it would be a sort of national referendum and a nation-wide exercise in solidarity that would unify the people. He works two years in the plantations of both the north and south coast, planning and organizing the strike. After this he returns to the capital to contact the members of the old conspiracy; through them he hopes to enlist support for the strike among the business and professional classes.

To get in touch with these men in spite of police surveillance, he learns the trade of ash collecting from an Indian. It consists in buying wood ash from private homes (and cleaning out their furnace in the process) in order to sell it to a soap factory at a small profit. This is the means of livelihood for some of the city Indians. Sansur adopts the demeanor, the speech, and the short, running gait of an Indian, and with his features obscured by the ashen mask of his new trade, he is able to circulate freely through the city streets and to penetrate un-observed into the homes of his former associates. Like a phoenix rising from the ashes, he makes his appearance before these men who had thought him dead and presents them with his proposition. These interviews with business and professional men offer Asturias the opportunity to illustrate the attitude of the country's social and intellectual elite toward the strike and toward the new social structure it may inaugurate. On the whole they agree to uphold and promote the strike, although they think it cannot work. But there are some who reject Sansur's plan altogether because it would be the beginning of socialism. Everybody would want to get into the act; the common people would think they had a right to give orders; and who would take charge of the government?

Sansur calls this drawing fire from the ashes. Indeed, re-curring references to ashes, sparks, embers, and fire symbolically develop the relationship between the dictatorship and the revolution. Years of tyranny have snuffed out the spirit of a people: their initiative and solidarity lie dead or dormant under the clammy dust of terror that each dictator spews forth for his own protection. Some smoldering embers burst into flame here and there, student demonstrations, assassination plots; but their sparks fall on dead ash and they are quickly stamped out. Sansur's slow and dangerous task is to burrow into this ashpit, to revivify the remnants of trade guilds and their mutual responsibilities, to stir up residues of democracy, memories and dreams of freedom; in short, to ready the city bourgeois, the laborers, and the agricultural workers for a zero hour when a spark will ignite the whole population, setting it ablaze with a nonviolent revolution. Then the rebirth of the nation can be achieved without bloodshed. Nonviolence! A new weapon for Latin Americans and the only one against which dictators are unarmed. In promulgating nonviolence in detail, Asturias provides an unexpected outlet for the mounting hatred he illustrates in the course of the trilogy; he may have been the first to introduce this philosophy into Latin American literature. By arguing that revenge and destruction of the company may be temporarily gratifying but their harmful results devolve upon the workers, Sansur sets an example to future generations.

When finally the zero hour has come and gone, and the President has resigned; when Sansur has curbed the violence of thousands of machete-wielding field workers and, after agonizing days the company has recognized the workers' syndicate, the reader is stunned by the modesty of the people's victory. They have won only the barest justice: the right to form a union and to negotiate a work contract. The cataclysm envisioned in *Viento fuerte*, both by the Indians and by visiting Americans, has become, under the guidance of Octavio Sansur, the foundation of a new society promising freedom and dignity to the workers. The welcome anticlimax emphasizes, of course, the grossness of former injustices.

I   *The Generation Gap*

Early in the book Sansur tries to enlist Juambo's help in organizing the strike. As GMT's confidential servant, Juambo could provide valuable information; his background would seem to fit him for revolutionary work: his parents were among the dispossessed of the Atlantic coast, whose leader had been the Indian Chipo Chipó. Yet there is little understanding between Sansur and Juambo. Sansur is the man of action who works for an objective ideal, the betterment of man, not the passive sufferer of grievances that Juambo is. He is dedicated to putting his ideas into effect for the benefit—not of himself (he is rootless) but of his country. As far as Juambo is concerned there is no mana about Sansur, no mystery. The shadowy figure of Chipo Chipó, symbol of resistance, has more appeal to him even now than the blunt and practical Sansur. Chipo had sacrificed himself (and others) in the Motagua River thus sealing his leadership and pathetic protest. This was more meaningful to Juambo than the prosaic plan of this new leader.

Besides, there is the question of land restitution. Sansur has no real concept of the land mystique—he was a city urchin—but to Juambo this is more important than any abstract betterment of the worker. Hoping to win him, Sansur repeats that the hour will come to recover the land—or its value, and he does not seem to realize that to be paid could never answer Juambo's psychic needs (Maker Thompson had been willing to *pay*), which demand the restitution of a particular parcel of land now lost among acres of banana trees. Juambo cannot grasp that the problem now concerns the thousands of workers who have since been sucked into the plantations and that, until justice can be meted to them, the matter of lands must be shelved. Once again Asturias dramatizes the psychic truth of myth which can have more weight than reality. Juambo, the logical material for a rebel but lost to the cause due to a psychological block, epitomizes the obstacles that mark Sansur's progress toward awakening the social conscience of Guatemalans. In dealing with the staid middle class Sansur encounters more setbacks, but those who cause them are not as guiltless as poor Juambo.

II   *Interpretative Notes*

Providing the love interest is Malena Tabay, a rural school-teacher who comes to share Sansur's vision and revolutionary objectives. From a mawkish and lachrymose young woman, she is changed by the contagion of his idealism and their mutual love into an effective leader, one who can harangue the crowds in Guatemala City. It may be that through her the author intended to give form to the surprising change that occurred among schoolteachers as a body during that era: from the meekest civil employees, they became leaders of the uprising.

Throughout his novels Asturias has created a lively gallery of feminine characters: garrulous women of the people of all ages and dispositions, rich and avaricious old bigots, sweet, innocent girls like Camila, dreamers like Mayarí. But except for Leland Foster who is highly convincing as a mature woman in love, he has not yet provided his protagonists with companions of their stature. In *Hombres de maíz*, where woman is the dominant subject, she is seen from the viewpoint of man; by and large this can also be said of his other works. Apparently he is not interested so much in women as such as in their effect upon the masculine world, reflecting the psychological fact that man's experience of them is dominated by the psychic projection of his anima.

Malena Tabay has a role that would be comparable to Leland's but as a character she is not as appealing as she is probably meant to be. One could wish for more composure in the counterpart of Sansur. She has multiple roles to play, however, which may account for some of her quirks. Besides personifying the pusillanimity of the teaching profession and its conversion to political action, she evidently represents another indigenous goddess, Xtabay, as her name and several descriptions of her suggest. Thus, her copious tears may be explained as sympathetic magic to produce rain. Sansur likewise has many divine characteristics, including his assumed name, Mondragón (dragon, symbol of the agrarian god); his sojourn in the underground cave could be studied as a replica of the sun's career. His venereal disease, mentioned fleetingly, and the fact of his rising anew from the ashes, recall a legend of the sun.[1]

Los ojos is somewhat disappointing after the high quality of the first four novels of Asturias. Perhaps it could bear some abridgment of the strike details. Nevertheless, it is a competent book; its greatest value comes from its minute and vivid portrayal of the social texture of Guatemala in the early 1940's.

III   *Conclusion of the Trilogy*

I have not stressed the correlation of the trilogy novels with factual events because the author has obviously not intended to place them in any historical context. In the matter of dates, for example, there is hopeless confusion: Boby Thompson was conceived at the time his grandfather, GMT, was in Chicago conferring on the question of annexation, six or eight years after the annexation of Hawaii, says the text, therefore in 1906 at the latest; yet Boby is only an adolescent during the revolution, presumably thirty-eight years later. Again: during that revolution, which occurred, historically speaking, in June, 1944, Aurelia talks of Hiroshima as of a past event, although it did not happen until August 1945.

One of the reasons why critics belabor the social authenticity of the novels is to demonstrate that Asturias has not exaggerated, which can certainly be done. The significance of the Banana Trilogy as a piece of literature, however, does not rest in the crimes committed by the fruit company, which, after all, is depicted as the impersonal monster that it is, but in the effect of such crimes on individuals or on groups of sentient human beings. It is, therefore, of small consequence whether this or that crime is factual or not, as long as it is credible, and no informed reader should have difficulty in accepting without proof the premise that monopolies often use unconscionable methods. Although from a nonliterary viewpoint the social thesis is a matter of utmost importance both to Asturias and to any civilized person, it is evident from the large proportion of material unrelated to these problems which the author introduces into his texts, that he would not entirely reject my stance. "I have often been criticized, particularly in the Socialist countries, for dwelling on mythical aspects, thereby diluting my social indictments and the impact of reality. I can only reply that the impotent scribbling called

Socialist Realism is worthless to me. More important, my novels are realistic precisely because they do include these aspects."[2]

What is authentic in the three novels, irrespective of details, is the author's interpretation of the spirit during the first half of the century. Rightly or not, the huge banana enterprise has aroused the hostility of a large segment of the people, even among those who benefit from it. Estrada Cabrera, who brought it into Guatemala, is portrayed by Asturias as saying that he had worked to save the country from the piracy of the Americans. Various shades of hatred and antagonism make up a substantial element of the psychological climate both in Central America and, translated into fictional terms, in these books.

Furthermore, it is difficult to see why the trilogy should ever be considered anti–American. The author does not pick Americans to be his villains. On the contrary, his vilest characters are invariably Guatemalans—police officials, army officers, traitors, and cowards—whereas Americans are among the noblest: Leland and Lester Mead, and GMT is interesting because he is not all bad. Or is it because the company in question happens to be American? But American antitrust laws have recognized the evils that Astruias denounces and tried to correct them in our own country. These are American problems, but to write about them does not make one anti-American. Are we prepared to call Steinbeck anti-American for *The Grapes of Wrath*? Dos Passos? Dreiser? Sinclair? Norris? No, there is no exposé of unjust business tactics in the books of Asturias that has not had its equivalent in our own literature.

CHAPTER 9

His Five Dramas

THE Spanish American theater traces its origins to indigenous plays which in pre-Columbian times were performed
all over the continent. In a broad sense all Indian dances,
including those still executed today, are expressions of the
strong dramatic impulse of the Amerind. For example, the
fertility dance called *palo volador*, in which one performer
dances on a minuscule platform atop a high pole, while others
fly through space tied to the pole by their legs, expresses the
cosmic intercourse of heaven and earth (as did the erection of
a stele for the ancient Maya and the erection of the *djed* in
ancient Egypt), and each participant, having prepared for
the occasion by a general fast, has divested himself of his
own personality and assumed the identity which his role in
the drama demands.

To a much greater degree, the numerous rituals which acted
out the major functions of the gods, were highly theatrical.
Among the Aztecs, the young woman who was to be decapitated
and flayed in honor of Toci, *was* Toci and she was honored as
such during the time preceding her sacrifice; the youth who
then donned her skin became thereby the corn god, Centeotl:
he *was* the grain of corn in the womb of the earth. Many of
the songs and chants pertaining to such festivals have come
down to us.

It is believed that there were also performances which had
been formally conceived as drama; like the medieval mysteries
and miracle plays, they were not strictly part of the religious
cult but an extension of it. The only such play surviving from
the pre-Hispanic theater is the drama-ballet *Rabinal Achí*
(The Man of Rabinal), also called "Dance of the Drum."
The Maya Quiché text was discovered in the mid-nineteenth

century and later studied and translated by Georges Raynaud, Miguel Angel Asturias' professor at the Sorbonne.

Rabinal Achí concerns a valiant and high-ranking warrior who is taken prisoner by his equally noble enemy, and partakes of certain rites and ceremonial dances in preparation for the ineluctable dénouement: sacrifice by removal of his heart. At first contact the play seems static and the antiphonal parallelism of the dialogue is tiringly repetitious; but to the Maya, the question of boredom or excitement does not arise, for to him, time is sacred. The past is indistinguishable from the present or the future. Stimulation is not a criterion for judging his entertainments.

As a spectacle, the beauty of *Rabinal Achí* depended largely on the wealth of dazzling plumes, ornaments and other accountrements that the performers could muster, which in pre-Conquest days is known to have been fabulous. Nevertheless, the play continued to be performed for another three hundred years (until independence from Spain), long after the Indians had been reduced to servility and poverty; obviously its magic did not depend solely on pageantry.

The power of the drama-ballet resides not in its action but in its style. Its persistent repetitions, its rhythmic dances and drums undoubtedly helped to carry the participants, dancers and audience alike, outside themselves and into a state of trance or semiconsciousness.[1] At the same time, *Rabinal Achí* depicts ceremonies leading to and, no doubt in its original form, including sacrifice. In this respect, it satisfied the need for the experience of sacrifice and must have been especially valuable to the post-Conquest Indians (to whom any thought of their old sacrifices was forbidden) in that it retained the image that expressed so basic an unconscious factor. Thus, we have at least two reasons for the success of *Rabinal Achí* with its intended audience, which would not be immediately apparent to the civilized theatergoer of today.

During the Colony, the Spanish priests who sought to bring Christianity to the Indians fostered their dramatic aptitude for its excellent educational and proselytizing value. They encouraged the natives to act out allegories about good and evil, episodes from the Bible, and other such things. Amidst

the many traditional plays and pageants that are still enacted
by the descendants of the Mayas, one of the most charming
and yet poignant dramatizations was recently discovered—
poignant because of the utter incomprehension it reveals to
have existed between the two races, the American and European. Under the guise of biblical pageants, the Chortí Indians
of eastern Guatemala re-enact episodes from the *Popol Vuh*.
What they call the "Dance of the Giants" consists of two parts,
the beheading of St. John the Baptist, and the struggle between
David and Goliath. Dr. Rafael Girard, the Swiss anthropologist,
attended many performances which, as a privileged friend,
he was allowed to photograph, and he has provided an engrossing analysis of its meaning.

Although the actors and producers of the drama have no
direct knowledge of the *Popol Vuh* as we know it, nor presumably of the Bible, Dr. Girard was able to recognize the
decapitation of Hun Hunahpú by the Lords of the Underworld
in the St. John episode, and the fight of the young sun god
with the same forces of evil, in the David-and-Goliath sequence,
which indeed it somewhat resembles. The entire spectacle is
formally dedicated to "el Rey," the sun; at the beginning and
end of each performance the actors salute the sun by swinging
their swords (sunrays) in a semicircle from east to west, following its path through the skies. Thus, traditional legends of
pre-Hispanic culture have endured and survived nearly five
hundred years of suppression.[2]

All of these dramas, *palo volador*, *Rabinal Achí*, and the
"Dance of the Giants," are related to the plays of Asturias
by virtue of their common historical and geographical origins,
but I have described them in some detail for another more
important reason. None of them depend on narrative interest
nor on visual form for their justification, but rather on their
hidden meaning and on their inner form. *Palo volador* is more
than graceful feats of equilibrium, it is a symbolic way of
expressing a great unknowable process, the mystery of generation. The "Dance of the Giants," too, means something
deeper than its apparent plot; it gives form to the undying
theme of sacrifice. So does *Rabinal Achí*, and *palo volador*
is not far removed from that theme either. More significantly,

what has made all three dramas powerful and effective for their audiences is the fact that they appeal directly to unconscious factors rooted in the human psyche.

Except in one historical play, Asturias is also more interested in the underlying truths his plays express than in the plots and characters.

I   Cuculcán

The persistent vitality of Maya myths, such as that shown by Dr. Girard, supports Asturias' view that "when we speak of myths we speak of a living thing";[3] it contradicts the Western tendency to dismiss them for being "untrue," or at best to consider solely their artistic value. Asturias contends that the world in which the Indian lives is unknown and not even suspected by most other Guatemalans, although they share the same habitat; because the world that the Indian experiences is filled with fellow beings, animals, plants, mountains and lakes, fire and earth, sun, moon and stars, giants and dwarfs, each alive, each endowed with a spirit, each regarded by the Indian with eternal expectancy and among whom he feels himself to be an intruder. In other words, the Indian projects the contents of his unconscious upon his world, with which he feels a psychic identity (*participation mystique*).

In trying to convey his exceptionally perceptive understanding for the world of the Indian, Asturias has variously proceeded, approaching the subject in more or less direct terms. *Cuculcán* is a piece in which he concedes nothing to European frames of reference, although a few explanatory notes do accompany it. It is written in dramatic form, but the author has not included it in his collection of plays; instead, it is generally published as an appendix to his first book of tales, *Leyendas de Guatemala*. The text of the play is about seventy pages long and calls for much dancing and singing.

Cuculcán draws on the *Popol Vuh* and the *Annals of the Cakchiquels*, as well as on the Yucatecan books of *Chilam Balam*; the latter are writings of a mystic and symbolic nature, containing prophecies, riddles, and initiation procedures; they are among the most recondite of all Maya records.

Cuculcán might best be described as a chromatic ballet based on the three daily positions of the sun: morning, afternoon, and night, with corresponding stage settings and costumes of yellow, red, and black. The two principal characters are Cuculcán, one of the supreme gods (a spelling Asturias prefers over the usual Kukulkán as being more appropriate to Spanish which has no letter *k*) and Guacamayo, the mythical Vukub Cakix, a false god and deceiver; the latter is a macaw, clothed in all the colors of the rainbow and called "Rainbow of Deceit." Secondary characters are other folkloric beings, a flower, a dwarf grandmother, the wind (heard, not seen), hummingbirds, turtles, and archers who are probably potencies of the sun, because sunbeams are often conceived as arrows.

The language is of great poetic beauty, suggesting the ineffable, although the meaning of the whole might not be possible to pinpoint. Guacamayo contends that life is an illusion, a motionless dream, and that nothing is real; what we see is only a mirage to which the movement of the passing sun seems to give life. He asserts that nothing exists other than the sun, and while other creatures know him to be a deceiver, he creates a doubt in Yaí's mind. She is a yellow flower (or she may be the moon), and she asks Cuculcán, Lord of Heaven and Earth, to tell her where the succession of days and nights is leading. It seems to lead nowhere. It creates a feeling of movement which does not exist, because the only one who moves is he, the sun; it creates a feeling of life, which is not real but fictitious; and even as a fiction life is not hers, she adds, because she and all the world are figures in a dream: corporeal dreams that belong to their dreamer.

A briefer summary of *Cuculcán* has been made by another Guatemalan playwright, who describes it as the advent, plenitude, and setting of the sun "amid the voices that people Nature and daily manifest their amazement at the phenomenon of passing time."[4]

II   Soluna

Since 1955 Asturias has published four plays which are of a more conventional nature. The first, *Soluna*, is a modern miracle play in which Maya Indian beliefs take the place of Christian ones. The "miracle" happens through a medicine mask belonging to an Indian sorcerer called Soluna. He never appears on stage, but his presence is felt throughout, and his name, combining the words *sol* and *luna*, is the key to the miracle and to the play. The plot, laid in present-day Guatemala, recalls sections of *Hombres de maíz*; again we have the story of a man whose wife has left him, but set this time in a middle-class milieu. Ninica, born and bred in the city, is the recent bride of the owner of a country estate, Mauro. They married with the agreement that she will be free to return to city life if she finds rural living uncongenial. The play begins as she is leaving for the capital, and Mauro tries pathetically to delay her without actually breaking his promise; but it develops that her train is derailed and in the end she returns, telling her husband that their pact is canceled and that they will begin all over again.

The main interest, however, centers on the husband, and the envy he feels for his servants and other country folk: in a crisis, their faith in supernatural powers sustains them, while he, who cannot share their beliefs, is fearful and helpless at this critical crossroads of his life. His anguish has driven him to visit the local shaman and confide that his wife was bent on leaving him. Soluna, the sorcerer, gave him a medicine mask having the virtue of making time pass quickly; it will help Mauro wait until Ninica returns . . . or until he forgets her.

Soluna's mask now hangs prominently on the wall of Mauro's living room, where the play unfolds. The mask is half orange, half yellow, a composite of the sun and the moon, just like the name of its owner. It conveys graphically the conjunction of the two celestial bodies and Maya belief is that when the sun and the moon come together in an eclipse, years can slip by in minutes, centuries in hours, in accordance with the long-standing detachment of Maya philosophers from the constrictions of time. The presence of this magic object has been causing some uneasiness in the house, especially to Porfirio, a farm hand, who stands in deep awe of Soluna's powers, and has learned that this very night an eclipse is due to occur.

Waiting for supper to be served, Mauro is musing over these things as he takes the mask off the wall and examines it. Presently he falls asleep in his armchair. He dreams that he puts the mask on and as he does the room is suddenly flooded with daylight; he takes it off and it becomes dark again. He continues to do this, making the light flash on and off, when he hears drums and shouts approaching, and four groups of dancers burst in one after the other; two groups are partisans of the moon and two of the sun. Taking turns, they chant, call on their respective god, and perform, arrayed and lighted in appropriate color schemes: yellow light and green costumes for the moon people, white light and red outfits for the sun. After their parallel and alternate dances, the two factions start fighting in a stylized manner, each side trying to displace the other from the center of the stage. Taken as a whole, this sequence can be seen as an encounter between the sun and the moon, in other words, an eclipse, transposed into the idiom of dance.

The ballet is ended abruptly by the arrival of Porfirio announcing that the end of the world is at hand: horses, oxen, and the village church bell have fallen in a ravine. At someone's command, all the people begin to group themselves on the right of the stage avoiding the left side, in reference to Judgment Day when the sheep will be on the right hand and the goats on the left. During the shuffle a voice declares that it is all the fault of a gypsy woman who caused the eclipse by predicting it; the mob is incensed and prepares to start after her and kill her with their machetes, when in walks Ninica.

Mauro, who has taken no part in his own dream, now runs joyfully to welcome her. In the hush that follows, Ninica draws attention to the fact that the church bell is ringing again, whereupon everybody shouts "Miracle! Resurrection! We live again!"[5] The dream ends and we return to Mauro dozing on his chair. Soluna's mask has fallen at his feet. The maid comes in with supper just in time to see a fantastic animal, like a coyote, slink in the front door, snatch the mask, and run off with it in its jaws. Her screams awaken Mauro; he hears the animal howling outside, grabs his shotgun, and fires into the dark, but the maid tears the weapon from his hands: "Don't shoot . . . it's Porfirio! It's the *nahual* of Porfirio!" (p. 172). The proof of it, she adds, is that the mask is gone. Perplexed, Mauro goes out and calls Porfirio by name, but there is no answer.

All that remains of the play is a short finale: later that night, when the house is asleep, the very people Mauro saw in his dream knock at the door with news of the wrecked train. They bring Ninica on a stretcher. People were out to see the eclipse, making noise to help the moon against the sun, following Indian custom, therefore many were on hand to help the passengers. When Ninica regains consciousness, she tells Mauro that she is a changed woman and that now she will not leave him again.

Porfirio returns briefly, bringing back the mask. His arm is wrapped in bloodstained rags. He complains that somebody shot him earlier when he came for the mask; he wanted to take it away to break the spell that was on the house. Mauro turns to his wife and asks, is this still a dream? "No, my love, we are awake now. Day is breaking, and for me it's like the first day of the world" (p. 178). A world has ended and a new world begins. The curtain falls as the first rays of the sun burst in upon them.

Here, as in *Hombres de maíz*, a man caught in an emotional crisis to which there is no solution short of a miracle, turns instinctively to the irrational for help. Mauro is a typical modern, adrift from the beliefs and collective symbols of his culture (Catholicism in his case) but with so pressing a need for its archetypal patterns that he deliberately attempts to inject himself into the parallel structure of Indian beliefs by seeking out the sorcerer, Soluna. This step toward the irrational is an invitation to his unconscious to make itself heard, which it promptly does through a dream. According to the experience of Jungian psychoanalysts, dreams have become the principal channel by which the unconscious can guide civilized man through his problems.

Mauro needs new strength to surmount his situation: an act of renewal is in order. It was seen, in connection with *Hombres de maíz*, that the essence of renewal is sacrifice, real or symbolic, whereby consciousness gives up an instinctive

drive or libido to the unconscious in order to regain it in renewed form. The union of opposites (conscious and unconscious)
produces new psychic energy.[6] In Mauro's dream, elements
of death, sacrifice, and rebirth are discernible. Death is signified
in a general way by Porfirio's announcement of the world's
end; sacrifice to the Great Mother is implied by the loss of
animals and bell down the ravine, because the first represent
animal instincts, and the bell, higher impulses, which by
disappearing into the bosom of mother earth (the Great Mother)
are sacrificed to the unconscious. Outright sacrifice is proposed
when the peasants decide to kill the gypsy woman. Rebirth
is signified by the ringing bell (thought to be dead), which
draws the cries of resurrection from the peasants. Rebirth
is also suggested at the end when Ninica tells Mauro that
she is a new woman; the girl who ran off this morning is gone
for good, she explains; she was a city girl and not wholly
Mauro's anyway, but the one who has come back is his true
country wife. Together, they will start life over again.

III   Soluna *as a Stage in Psychic Development*

Jung explains that for those who experience it, individuation
begins when a person realizes that consciousness, of which
the ego is the center, does not represent the whole personality,
and he turns toward a deeper reality, toward those traits of
his psyche that have hitherto remained hidden from him.
Knowingly or not, he is searching for psychic wholeness, for
the center of that which embraces the conscious *and* the unconscious and is termed the Self. Mauro is thirty-three, traditionally the age of Christ when he died and resurrected,
and for that reason significant; besides, it is close to the halfway
mark through life; he is therefore at the age when individuation
may begin.

A marked pattern of polarity is worked into his dream,
reproducing the sun-and-moon theme. The flashing lights at
the beginning as he puts the mask on and off, and later, the
veritable battle of lights during the struggle between the four
groups of dancers, all portray the activation of light and
dark, conscious and unconscious elements of human nature.
According to Jung, a living tension between consciousness and

the unconscious maintains our psychic balance and regulates the flow of psychic energy. This polarity characterizes the entire course of our existence, but it becomes more pronounced when we face the task of uniting the opposites, namely, of reconciling outer with inner reality. In Mauro's dream, the dancers are grouped in pairs of opposites; they perform alternately, and even their clothes, red or green, are complementary colors from the opposite sides of the spectrum. Other characters are described in like manner: a white-haired ox driver is coupled with a young, black-haired one; a Spaniard with a flowing white beard is married to a Creole with black tresses; a fierce, dark-complexioned peasant with black mustaches is teamed with a young, smiling one wearing a pale green hat. The detailed descriptions of these minor characters can serve no purpose other than to point up their contrasts. Furthermore, much stress is laid on the left hand versus the right hand in the Last Judgment scene, as well as in a palmistry episode with the gypsies, thereby picking up the binary pattern on another level and conveying the same meaning. The left (sinister) points to the unconscious, and the right (dexter, auspicious) to the opposite. The moon (feminine) and the sun (masculine) have similar connotations. As these pairs of opposites move about the stage, clashing, contrasting, each dominating our attention in turn, they suggest the alternating action of intuition and intellect, of matter and spirit, body and soul, magic and science, and of all the opposite drives that provide the rhythm and dynamics of life.

When, by delving into the unconscious, one attempts to bring some of its contents to light, a temporary imbalance occurs, as portrayed by Mauro's crisis. But the effort leads, or should lead, to the creation of a new stability, based on a self-knowledge that brings together the rational and the irrational worlds. In the play, where Mauro stands for the rational and his flighty wife for the irrational (he calls her *mi animalito*, my little animal, as a term of affection), this stability is established by their reunion and the promise of their future togetherness.

The first archetypal figures to be met in the course of individuation are those Jung calls the shadow and the anima. The shadow, representing repressed attributes of the ego of which consciousness is unaware or refuses to acknowledge, is often experienced as a person of our sex whom we consider somewhat inferior. In *Soluna*, Porfirio personifies Mauro's shadow: he has the primitive, spontaneous characteristics that are the counterpart, the reverse side of a reasonable, sensible man such as Mauro is. Insofar as the *nahual* of Porfirio is wild and fearsome it symbolizes the animal impulses and instinctive drives that may erupt from the unconscious when its contents are deliberately activated as at this time.[7]

The anima is the image of the other sex that we carry within us around which our suppressed feminine traits have clustered; it is normally projected upon the beloved or some other desirable object. But when a man recognizes that this femininity is an aspect of his own psyche, he naturally withdraws the projection. It is as if a figure on a motion-picture screen were suddenly to disappear. Asturias has expressed this situation more than once through the image of a disappearing wife—an appropriate metaphor because a wife would ordinarily be the one to carry the projection of the anima. In *Hombres de maíz* he coined the word *tecuna* after the character María Tecún to denote such a runaway wife, and the term is used in *Soluna* to describe Ninica. Her departure indicates to us that Mauro no longer projects his anima on her; if he can assimilate this aspect of his unconscious, that is to say, if he recognizes that the feminine characteristics he experienced objectively are actually his own, his consciousness will expand and he will mature accordingly. This he does when, after the eclipse, he welcomes Ninica back to a new, permanent union.

Along with the anima, there frequently appears the archetype of the wise old man, whose chief function is to give advice. In *Viento fuerte* this figure was projected by Lino on the shaman who cured him of his anima troubles. It is a personification of the Self, and because it represents the whole personality, male and female components inclusive, it is often androgynous (combining both sexes). In *Soluna*, this figure is the shaman from whom Mauro sought advice. The sorcerer's name, which combines the archetypal symbols of the sexes, Sol-Luna, indicates that he is androgynous. Soluna's mask provoked Mauro's dream, which in turn allowed the tensions of opposites in his psyche to resolve themselves, while affording him a personal version of the death-and-rebirth ritual, the preliminary step of individuation. Insofar as a *nahual* is a helpful guardian spirit, it symbolizes the Self, and in the play Porfirio's is helpful in removing the "spell" from Mauro.

Among many other graphic representations of the Self, the most common are the circle, the center, and the number four; these frequently occur in symmetrical patterns representing wholeness and balanced harmony. When the dancers in the dream push each other from the center of the stage, following Asturias' directions, they must move around the center forming a *circular* or symmetrical pattern. At any rate, the movement of the *four* groups of performers converges toward the *center*, and this centripetal motion toward a point of stability culminates in the eclipse.

The eclipse is the climax of the drama on all levels. In the surface plot it brings inner security to Mauro by giving Ninica back to him. Psychologically, an eclipse is the union of opposites, the *coniunctio* or sacred marriage of Sol and Luna, which in the Middle Ages was the goal of alchemists. By combining the conscious and unconscious, light and dark, masculine and feminine components of the psyche, a total, balanced personality is achieved, such as is signified by the dancing hermaphroditic figure of Shiva and Shakti. In the play, this meaningful union is well expressed and symbolized by the two halves of Soluna's mask, which denote the wholeness we strive for through the process of individuation.

IV   La audiencia de los confines

The expression that Asturias uses as the title of his next play, *La audiencia de los confines* (1957), is the name by which the most remote courts of justice were known under the Spanish empire. It may be roughly translated as "Tribunal of the Frontiers."

The play is about the sixteenth-century humanitarian and political theorist, Bishop Bartolomé de Las Casas. It dramatizes the moral triumph of the "Apostle to the Indians," as he came to be called, when he returned to Guatemala from the

court of Spain bringing with him the New Laws for the protection of the Indians. In 1542, upon the recommendation of
the Bishop and other advisors, Emperor Charles V decreed
the New Laws. Among other things, they abolished the semi-
feudal *encomienda* system, whereby the Spanish colonist had
the right to exact tribute from the Indians assigned to him,
and therefore they put an end to Indian slave labor. They
were received with less than enthusiasm by the colonists who
deemed the project of colonization to be impossible if the New
Laws were enforced, and who considered Las Casas, at best,
a meddling fool.

This was not the first effort that Las Casas had made on
behalf of the Indians. As far back as 1516 he had been officially
dubbed "Protector of the Indians" by the Spanish regent
Cardinal Cisneros; in 1521 he organized a peaceful colonization
in an attempt to win the Indians to Christianity by good
example; and in 1537 when he was sixty-three years of age,
he and three other Dominicans had begun the conquest of a
region of Guatemala inhabited by fierce Indians (Verapaz)
with no other weapon than the word of God.

Nor were the New Laws the friar's last endeavor to prevent
iniquities from being perpetrated upon the American natives.
In 1550 he challenged and debated one of the best trained
scholars of the Emperor's court, Ginés de Sepúlveda, who
contended that Spaniards were justified in subjugating the
Indians because these were barbarians and by nature inferior.
To which Las Casas retorted that far from being inferior, the
culture attained by American Indians was equal and often
superior to that of the pagan Greeks and Romans; that their
moral virtues were such that Spaniards would do well to copy
them; and that the pyramids of the Maya compared favorably
with those of Egypt. At the age of ninety he was still bringing
out controversial treatises bearing on the rights of infidels;
indeed, the cell to which he had retired was so crowded with
his manuscripts that it was difficult to get in and out of it.[8]

It was inevitable that Asturias would not forever resist the
appeal of a figure so like himself; Las Casas was in many
ways his own precursor; and so it happened that the Bishop,

to whom he has referred as a veritable Quixote, prompted his only sally, so far, into the field of history.

The first act of *La audiencia de los confines* features a divided stage with the action shifting from the Governor's headquarters in Guatemala on one side, to an Indian temple containing a statue of the corn god on the other. The New Laws deprived the colonists of their slaves and therefore of their status as gentlemen. They would not go into effect until Bishop Las Casas arrived with them from Spain, but long before that the Spaniards of the colonies had begun fighting them. Another cause of grievance against the Bishop was his decree that absolution be withheld from all persons who owned Indian slaves.

The lust and duplicity of the Governor is soon established; his concern centers not on the acquisition of gold so much as on the enjoyment of Indian maidens, whose untamed and elemental charms have become his engrossing passion. Through deception and intrigue he has been secretly trafficking in young girls dedicated to the corn god, arousing the wrath of native priests and warriors. The latter, under the leadership of a woman, Naborí, mistakenly suspect one of their own people and trust the Governor; their disillusionment will provide the climax of the drama.

The Governor sends a Dominican friar to the Indians on a peace mission and contrives to have them slay him. Pretending to lament the priest's death, he turns it into propaganda against Las Casas' theories. Meanwhile the Spanish settlers are in a turmoil over the expected arrival of Las Casas; they mean to capture "the wicked bishop" and ship him to Peru, where he is even more hated, because he endangers their salvation by refusing them absolution. No one has the slightest intention of giving up their Indians.

In the third and last act Bishop Las Casas arrives, not escorted by armed guards as expected, but with no more company than his seventy years. He takes refuge in the episcopal palace, and convokes a meeting of government officials for the formal proclamation of the New Laws. The Governor dares not touch Las Casas openly. His plan is to have the

Indians, led by Naborí, descend upon the palace and attack Las Casas, whereupon his men, pretending to protect the bishop, will take him into custody and dispose of him. Naborí, who like all the Indians, loves the good bishop, now suspects the Governor of duplicity. She appears to cooperate with him, but when she and her Indian warriors swarm the palace it is to protect Las Casas and to urge him to escape with them. They fight off Spanish soldiers at the door of the palace, just off stage. Naborí is fatally wounded, but she has time to reveal the Governor's treachery. A royal judge arrests him in the name of the Tribunal of the Frontiers, and the curtain falls.

In reality the triumph of the Bishop was short-lived. It is not mentioned in the play, but less than two years later the New Laws were partially repealed. As we know, this did not discourage Las Casas who went on fighting for the rights of Indians until death overtook him at ninety-two.

Asturias tells that when this play was put on it Guatemala in 1961 it caused a lively controversy: a number of critics censured him for putting anachronisms into the Bishop's mouth, but he showed that on the contrary he had invented nothing. He had merely transcribed the words, slightly modernized, that Las Casas himself had written.[9] Asturias does not say which particular passage of the play was questioned, but most likely it was a dream sequence where the friar expresses his political theories. In his dream he found himself in the presence, of Charles V once again, repeating what he had told him: "Kings do not have absolute power by which to transfer vassals, towns and jurisdictions, without the consent of the governed! The authority of kings, princes and magistrates derives from the will of the nation, and these may never consider themselves to be above the law! ... The kings of Spain have no right to make war on the Indians, nor to conquer them by force of arms" (p. 230). The stage directions describe him as standing with his fist on the table in the attitude and with the bearing of a member of the French Convention of 1792. *This* might be termed anachronistic, were it not a justifiable device to indicate by analogy how far in advance of his times was the Bishop's thinking. In point of fact, Las Casas' arguments raised grave doubts in the Emperor's mind regarding his right to conquer the New World, and they prompted him to suspend any further conquest until the matter could be settled. This was the origin of the great debate of 1550–51 between Sepúlveda and Las Casas which Asturias telescopes into the play as a thing of the past. Actually, the Bishop of Chiapas had left America in 1547 never to return.

The relevance of the four-hundred-year-old controversies to the work of Asturias is clear. To this day, many descendants of the Spaniards reject the friar's views regarding Amerindians, regardless of the ratification they have since received from the Declaration of Independence and the Rights of Man, not to mention Latin America's own wars of revolution. The evils which afflict Guatemala, and therefore Asturias, flow from this myopia.

La audiencia is the only play of Asturias so far that contains no dancing properly speaking. In a production, however, the fighting between the Indians and the offstage Spaniards could be effectively stylized into a ballet, since war and dance are closely associated in the Indian mind.

V   Chantaje

It is difficult to be sure just what *Chantaje* (Blackmail) is about because so many things take place that seem not to have any bearing on subsequent developments. There are over thirty speaking parts; the first act is laid in a covered street or gallery, just off the intersection of two big arteries in a city of the American tropics. The noise of the traffic, trucks, sirens, and screeching brakes is surpassed only by the blare of a loudspeaker advertising merchandise in the gallery's shop windows interspersed by jukebox music at full blast. A blind beggar stands in the gallery playing a violin and can be heard during an occasional lull in the din.

Periodically all the lights go out, plunging the show windows into darkness for an instant in preparation for a fresh burst of floodlights and new outpourings of advertising from the loudspeaker. People come and go; what seem to be desultory conversations are held; a song-and-dance number is performed.

The main argument, however, seems to concern Carola, a prostitute; Dantés, a business tycoon; and Atchis, a crippled policeman. At the end of the first act, Carola leads the blind-man away to help him cross the busy avenue. The sound of an accident is heard offstage, and Carola returns, not with the beggar but with the policeman who had been directing traffic at the intersection. His legs have been crushed by a hit-and-run driver. The second act is in the office of Dantés where Carola blackmails the multi-millionaire for $60,000. She was on the spot when the car hit the policeman and she recognized the driver to be Dantés, her lover; she has the evidence of his blood-spattered hubcap which she turns over to him in exchange for the cash. The money, she says, is to go to Atchis, the victim.

By Act III, Atchis is living with Carola and she has not given him the money after all. He has fallen in love with her, but he is also violently jealous because the accident has rendered him impotent. Meanwhile, Dantés is pulling off a big deal to gain control of the nation's oil wells. Learning that Carola is a secret agent of the dictator, and that she has access to government files, he offers her $600,000 for information that will clinch the deal for him. She agrees to obtain it for him, and they become friends again.

Still to be reckoned with is the jealousy of Atchis; catching Carola in the arms of Dantés, he throws a bottle of ink at her face. In the end he kills Dantés with a pistol in Carola's apartment, then calmly calls the police. "I did it out of jealousy," he tells Carola in answer to her question. "He was the one who mutilated you; you could give that reason to the police," she suggests. "No, it was because of jealousy." "Well, then, tell them that Dantés was defrauding the country of the oil-wells." "No, I killed him out of jealousy," he insists. And thereupon the play ends (pp. 68–69).

Dantés' manipulation of the press is an entertaining side issue. Of course, he controls the news about himself by virtue of his heavy advertising, but the new twist is that he even deceives the editors themselves by feeding them gossip and trivia about his family's social life to divert the public's attention while he finagles with the national oil wells; he also provides them with minor unfavorable releases about himself so that the newspapers will seem to be impartial when they support him on major issues.

Some of the ludicrous situations and inconsequential action of *Chantaje* seem to place it in the theater of significant absurdity characteristic of our times, raising the question of what its arcane meaning may be. Indications are that the chaos of sound and light at the beginning of the play is meant to denote the creation of the world. The opening lines, a dialog between two disembodied voices, suggest as much: "Let there be light!" "No, let there be noise!" (p. 9). Whereupon the first voice asserts that the noise of the creation of the world is heard again at the dawn of each day. This is a manner of alluding to the dawn of consciousness, which for each human being is like creation repeated all over again. Jung has observed that the world would continue in the night of nonbeing were it not that human consciousness gives it the second creation of objective existence.[10] It seems to me that the play is "about" just that, the birth of consciousness.

When out of the sea of chaotic traffic, Carola drags Atchis wailing on the stage, we have, in projected, sensible form, the psychological drama of the nascent ego emerging, small and impotent, from the sea of the unconscious (uroboros) into the matriarchal world dominated by the figure of the Great Mother. Supporting this initial interpretation are the facts from the play.

The flow of traffic is actually visualized as a sea by a poetic schoolteacher directly after the accident so that the connection between the traffic policeman and the sea is easily made. The name Atchis suggests the Maya Quiché word, Achí, meaning man, as was seen in connection with *Rabinal Achí*. In a literal sense, he is small (he uses a roller board to get around), and he is impotent. From the moment of his accident, or "birth," he is absorbed in Carola, she becomes everything to him, he lives with her just as the infantile ego is dominated by the Great Mother. It is said of Carola by one of her admirers that she is "divine"; like the Great Mother, she is a harlot who belongs to no man, but gives herself to any man; Carola is markedly independent; she also has unquestioned power due to her connection with the government. She is a mixture of kindness and ruthlessness; she saves Atchis' life, she fights for him against Dantés, but she also works with Dantés to obtain the oil wells and is his mistress. Thus Atchis has ambivalent feelings toward her, fierce love and a wish to hurt her. Dantés affectionately calls her Gatita (Kitten); the great cat goddess Bast was characteristically ambivalent, at once sustaining and destroying life. When introduced, Carola is described as if she were a naked figurine such as those by which primitives represent the Great Mother: under her black velvet dress she wears nothing; her thighs seem molded on a lathe (she is of wood!); the girl's nakedness is frequently evoked. In ancient times nakedness was a sign of anonymity, whereby ritual harlots assumed the transpersonal nature of the Great Goddess they incarnated.[11]

The blind man, seen only in the first act, probably stands for the embryonic ego, before consciousness. His lack of one sense represents the total insensibility of this stage: someone says that he is lucky to have eyes that see nothing and a heart that desires nothing, where all around there is so much to be desired. Carola presides over the birth of the ego, as it were, when she takes the blind man off stage to help him cross the street and returns in a moment with the moaning Atchis; pain is among the first signs of consciousness.

Dantés must personify the negative aspect of the Great Mother; Carola seesaws between the positive and the negative, but he is steadfastly adverse. He is party to the stultifying advertising of the stores, party to the deadening barage of journalistic trivia intended to dissipate attention, to prevent thinking. It was he who castrated Atchis: matriarchal castration is a mythological metaphor expressing the swamping of the immature ego by the unconscious because it involves loss of masculine consciousness.

Atchis becomes aware of Dantés some time after the accident: he is beginning to differentiate between the two opposite aspects of the Great Mother.

The next major step in this accelerated version of ego development is to slay the dragon (Terrible Mother) and free the princess (anima), namely, to master the fearsome aspect of the unconscious and to liberate its creative component which, projected on the beloved, inspires him to achievement.

This is what Atchis does when he slays Dantés; at this point Carola clearly becomes the anima. She does not reproach Atchis as, logically, she might; on the contrary, she upholds his action and makes herself his accomplice by suggesting ways for him to protect himself from the law. She is his inspiration. For his part, he proves that she is by insisting that he killed Dantés out of jealousy, which is to say, for her sake— to free her from his adversary so as to have her for himself. In phoning the police he gives his address: 163 Avenida de las *Palmas*—the palms which as a hero he has won.

In connection with the petroleum business, Dantés nicknames Carola Leo Petra, an anagram of *petróleo. Leo,* lion, another cat: the terrible form of Bast was the lion goddess Sekhet. *Petra,* stone, has often been venerated as the Great Mother, for example at Paphos. Together both names suggest the Sphinx; all have feminine connotations.

When the works of Asturias are reread in the context of their interpretations, there are always delightful discoveries to be made. One example: outside a bookstore in *Chantaje* a group of intellectuals are window shopping. Carola, on her beat, passes among them, but none of the men notice her. She walks away with the comment that intellectuals are all impotent. What this dramatizes is the common situation in which consciousness, losing its link with the unconscious, is unaware of its existence and disregards its most blatant manifestations. Thus, the intellectuals, standing for onesided consciousness, pay no attention to Carola, the anima and agent of the unconscious. The *impotency* of the *intellectuals* consists in that consciousness is no longer able to *unite creatively* with the unconscious to achieve wholeness. The personality becomes atrophied: it has lost its soul, which is the cultural crisis of our times.

VI   Dique seco

Dique seco (Dry Dock) is a two-act comedy set in the main hall or drawing room of a mansion belonging to the Marquess of Alconave, a grandee facing the classical comic situation of the impoverished nobleman who must outwit his creditors.

Neither his valet nor his porter have received any wages for
months. When the curtain rises the Alconave coat-of-arms is
shown magnified on a second curtain and surrounded by an
enormous lottery board. The escutcheon consists of a black
falcon perched upon a peninsula, over which the word AZAR
(Chance) is inscribed.

At the opening of the second curtain the Marquess of Alconave is found doing his morning exercises, clad in shorts
that reveal more bones than muscles. His friend Pichardino,
a mariner, drops in. The marquess welcomes him to his house
which, he smiles, is as high and dry as his friend's dry docks.
The mariner brings good news: in an ancient Roman ship
raised from the Tyrrhenian Sea, he has found a human bone,
a femur, with a secret compartment, and in it, a document
stating that Julius Caesar owed six million sestertia to one
Pichardino. The sole survivor of that family being the mariner
himself, experts have decreed that the Italian state is obliged
to settle the debt with him, to the sum of sixty million liras
in modern currency. Furthermore, he, Pichardino, will use the
money to pay off the marquess' creditors as soon as he receives
it, because Alconave has always treated him with the greatest
courtesy, as if he were a Sir Francis Drake among pirates,
while knowing him to be but a lowly caulker. The nobleman
cordially accepts the offer but only as a loan.

As the occasion is being celebrated with a bottle of port,
the marquess harkens to the street cry of a passing falconer,
summons the man to his presence and purchases from him a
black falcon, the hallowed emblem of the house of Alconave
(Alcon/ave means literally Falcon/bird). The price he pays
for the bird is one hundred and twenty pieces of gold, which
is nearly half the amount his valet has just collected from
the pawnshop for the purpose of placating the creditors.

Undismayed by the remonstrations of his servants, he names
the porter Chief Falcon Keeper and assures the valet that for
one of his lineage, falcons are and ever have been divine agents
of salvation and that the coming of the sacred bird into his
house is a good augury. Having "consulted" with the falcon,
he decides to send for his creditors and carefully prepares for
their arrival. They are to be seated around a large table over

which he will preside. His falcon keeper is to stand motionless on a balcony overhanging the hall holding the falcon on his left fist and a lance in his right.

At the beginning of Act II, all the townspeople who expect payment are seen pouring in the hall, chattering among themselves and with the valet who, at one point, is heard to observe that to settle accounts is like being born again. Alconave makes his entrance with ritual pomp and elegance. As he cannot pay them in full, he explains, he has decided to treat them to a game of lotto in which the prizes are two bags of gold pieces. The coins are but a foretaste of the gold bars he will soon receive and pass on to them.

The initial reluctance of the creditors to accept further deferment quickly breaks down before their gambling lust. Cards are distributed and the game begins, grains of corn being used for markers. But suddenly pandemonium breaks out because the marquess has dropped the remark that the gold bars will not derive from his mines in Transvaal, as rumored, but from Pichardino's sestertia, and everybody except the grandee knows that the mariner has been declared insane and locked up. Fighting and falling over one another, each creditor grabs as much of the magnificent furnishings as he can and hauls it away.

Cheerful and unperturbed, the marquess remains seated in his armchair while his house is ransacked. His character is best summed up by his own statement: "It is not that I am good-humored, but I always look for what is new in life, and the only thing that is really new is joy. Everything else is old" (Act II, p. 106).

Among his family heirlooms there is a relic, the mummified body of a holy ancestor, St. Placid, generally kept in a golden urn but hidden, before the onslaught of the creditors, in a suit of armor. The only one who has remained empty handed after the pillage is Padre Bonete, and since nobody has touched the armor, Alconave donates the ancestral relic to the padre's church in settlement of his debts to the priest; thus St. Placid's remains are reverently carried away in solemn procession.

The marquess had entertained the idea of marrying Princess Yolanda de Angola whose fortune would put him back afloat.

At the end of the play, he learns that Yolanda has entered the convent and left her fortune to him: at the same time, Pichardino, released from the insane asylum and in possession of the sixty million liras, discovers that the sea has flooded his dry dock and carried off the salvaged Roman ship which he had presented to his lordship of Alconave. The latter, whose serenity is no more affected by good news than by bad, receives him affectionately: "Who could help loving you, Mariner, not for your sestertia converted into liras, but because you have made a symbol out of reality. Your dry dock, flooded by the seas, symbolizes the dryness of this house, which is now inundated by the fortune of Princess Yolanda and by your liras. . . Never did I doubt that my good falcon would protect us. On the Alconave coat of arms stands the word 'Chance' [*Azar*] over a falcon perched on a peninsula in a field of doves; it is interpreted to be man, surrounded on all sides by the waters of possibility except on the side that links him with the Continent of Death" (Act II, pp. 115–16).

This gay adventure is interrupted by the coming and goings of Zerba, an "existential woman" attired in tight pants, and Jemmy Ross, a black band leader who wears clothes of the starkest white. He plays loud and hot jazz on the piano, then suddenly stops dead, tiptoes to the front of the stage, and whispers to the audience: "Do you hear the silence? Silence is jazz, too!" (Acts I, II, pp. 83, 114). At one point Jemmy offers the marquess a contract to join his band, whereupon His Lordship, who normally plays Beethoven and Chopin, sits down at the piano and executes a jazz piece with magnificent style.

Dique seco is an ebullient farce and like *Soluna* it has strikingly visual qualities. As in that earlier play, the contrast between light and darkness is greatly emphasized, beginning with the first stage directions which require that the values of the Alconave coat-of-arms (black falcon and white doves) be carried out in the decor: heavy dark furniture against draperies of white, "lunar" materials. The valet has a white jacket and black trousers, dark skin and white hair, and so on. As for auditory effects, all of Asturias' plays include obstreperous crowds at some point or other, but in *Dique seco*

his instructions are that the jazz be amplified throughout the
theater to the point of causing physical distress to the audience
—which makes Jemmy's sudden silence all the more effective.

Dique seco is the only work to date that Asturias has not
laid in Guatemala or thereabouts: although the locale is not
specified, it seems to be Italy.[12]

Given Asturias' propensity for incorporating the mythologies
of all races into his work, one is struck by the similarity of
Jemmy's expression "Silence is jazz," and the mystic Indian
syllable, *Aum*, which is expressed in four parts, *a, u, m* and the
subsequent silence. One might profitably pursue this lead
but among the mythological overtones that are apparent in
Dique seco, Egyptian ones predominate. For example, there
is a conspicuous similarity between the word on the Alconave
shield, Azar, and the original name of Osiris, As-ar. The hawk
which identifies the Alconave family is also the symbol of
Horus (which means hawk), the son and counterpart of his
father, Osiris. One of the prospective brides for the marquess
was called *Isis*andra (Isis was the wife of Osiris). When the
marquess prepares to withdraw to take a bath and get dressed,
Zerba declares that his bathtub looks like an Egyptian coffin
and that she is going with him to wash his back: there are
Egyptian murals that show Isis pouring water over the mummified body of Osiris, who is, among other things, the sacred
grain of corn. Isis, often depicted in a very narrow skirt down
to her ankles, actually looks as if she were wearing tight pants,
like Zerba. Also like Zerba, Isis is an "existential woman,"
not in terms of the modern philosophy, but in the sense that
all Great Mothers like herself are the source and sustenance
of existence.

Osiris, the sun and fertility god of Egypt, was twice overcome by his brother and adversary, Set (darkness). The first
time he was locked in a coffer and thrown into the Nile: his
grieving wife, Isis, rescued him and eventually brought him
back to life. The second time, Set dismembered Osiris' body
and scattered the pieces over the world: Isis sought and found
all the fragments except the phallus. For it, she substituted a
wooden phallus taken from the fertility ritual, which is a
symbol of spiritual regeneration.[13] As a result, Osiris became

the lord of the dead, the patron of rebirth, and his ritual became a pattern of psychic initiation; in addition, he retained control over agrarian fertility in his role as the personification of the Nile.

If we allow that the marquess is Osiris, the scene of the creditors stripping him of his family heirlooms would represent the dismemberment of Osiris by Set. The creditors would then stand for Set. This is supported in two amusing ways. First, by a play on words at the beginning of Act II, as the creditors are about to arrive. The voice of a barker is heard over a loudspeaker inviting people to gamble. He calls out numbers making a joke or a pun out of each one, and for seventy-two (*setenta y dos*) he says, "seten . . . tran dos," which may be read, "Set entrando(s)" (Set entering, p. 100). Indeed, the utterance has no other meaning.

The second way is by identifying creditors with executioners, which is essentially what Set was when he dismembered the body of Osiris: this is done as follows: the name of one of the creditors means scaffold (Patíbulo) because he comes from a long line of executioners; but he has left the profession and become a moneylender, which is another way of being an executioner, says one of the characters. For our purpose, all the marquess' creditors, who are moneylenders, are therefore executioners like Set. To make the allusion clearer, this man Patíbulo (or Bulopatí as he prefers it) is teased about trying to carry off a bust of Marie Antoinette, the way his headsman ancestor made off with the august head of that queen.

As soon as the play is considered in the light of the Egyptian myth, much additional evidence springs into view to confirm it. The first thing to mention is the matter of atmosphere. The rites and celebrations connected with the worship of Isis and Osiris were somewhat lewd or so they seem to our present way of thinking. In keeping with this tone there are several indelicate, if appropriate, puns and jests in the play; but perhaps more subtle than these is the pervading use that has been made of jazz. The word "jazz" is said to derive from a lewd expression meaning to copulate. Jazz dominates a great part of *Dique seco* and most fittingly so, because divine copulation and the resulting fertility is what the Osirian mysteries were all about.

Mummy is probably not the word a Catholic priest would apply to a saint's remains, as happens in the play, but it does have a definite Egyptian connotation. Here, the mummy of St. Placid brings to mind the original mummy after which all subsequent mummies were patterned, Osiris. The marquess is identified with St. Placid, being of the same family, besides which placid is an adjective that describes him well.

As the play begins, the marquess, doing his setting-up exercises, is pale, breathless and more bones than muscle, as becomes a mummy. One of his legs simply will not respond; Horus, who is one with Osiris, was weak in the legs. Lying on the floor and attempting to lift himself up, his lordship resembles the mummified Osiris, who also looks as if he might be exercising when shown at a forty-five degree angle in the act of resurrection.

During the Sed Festival of the Pharaohs, the king, who in life identified with Horus and in death with Osiris, dispensed food to the people: during the lottery the marquess distributes grains of corn to his guests as markers. At the Sed Festival a falcon was displayed publicly from a balcony: the marquess' falcon keeper stood on a balcony overlooking the hall, with the bird perched on his fist. An essential part of the Sed Festival was the raising of the *djed* signifying the resurrection of Osiris; St. Placid was raised from a supine to an erect position when he was taken from his golden urn and hidden in the suit of armor. Isis cut off the hand of Horus to cleanse it of pollution; the marquess says he would sooner let his hands be cut off than to play jazz—although with splendid inconsequence he gives an excellent jazz rendition later. Osiris had sun and moon affiliations; this would partly account for the stress on light and darkness in the play. The god had a black aspect and was called the Ethiopian (so did Isis). Jemmy, who has an affinity with the marquess, is probably his black counterpart. Princess Yolanda de Angola was imagined by Zerba to be black, and the latter pictured her own white body and Yolanda's ebony body lying on either side of the marquess on his nuptial bed: the light and the dark Isis.

One of the creditors claimed that she supplied the marquess with milk during seven months: that takes care of the Hathor (cow-headed) aspect of Isis; seven is the number most often associated with initiation. Alconave is said to be "like God"; his falcon is a "divine agent" (pp. 93, 97).

We saw in *Soluna* that Mauro was thirty-three, the climacteric age attributed to Christ at his death and resurrection. The marquess is also thirty-three, and what is more, in this play Asturias makes the point outright: when the barker calls out thirty-three he adds that it is the age of Christ. It may be said, psychologically speaking and without irreverence, that Osiris and Christ are manifestations of the same archetype, namely, the god who dies and comes back to life and who is the promise of every man's craving for immortality. There are several indirect references in *Dique seco* to rebirth, initiation, and to the night sea journey which, in Jungian psychology, is a figure of death and precedes rebirth. In the play mention is made of Jonas, whose adventure in the whale is one of the prototypes of the night sea journey. The valet says that to settle one's accounts is like being *born again*. The marquess states that in order to avoid being locked up in an insane asylum, Christopher Columbus "threw himself into the shadowy sea" (p. 108). Columbus' voyage of discovery certainly has all the makings of a typical night sea journey, having been a fearsome confrontation with death and the unknown (the Terrible Mother), followed by rebirth in the New World. But what is even more significant is the suggestion that Columbus undertook the journey in order to avoid insanity. Jungian psychology showed us, in connection with the María Tecún crag in *Hombres de maíz*, that sacrifice leading to renewal must be performed periodically lest grave mental disorders ensue, disorders that "sear and madden."

On two separate occasions the marquess compares his home to the mariner's dry dock; in the end we hear that the dry dock has been flooded. Now, mention of a flood in connection with Egypt immediately brings to mind the sacred flood waters of the Nile, upon which that otherwise dry land depended for the irrigation of its crop lands. Under these circumstances, perhaps the femur with the miraculous I.O.U. hidden within it, through virtue of which the marquess' home was flooded with the riches it sorely needed, is the ritual phallus of Osiris which brought the riches of fertility to the land of Egypt. (Egypt was the home of Osiris.)

Many additional clues or indicators may be found in the play, and more than one interpretation may be given to some of them. For example, the femur, which is the lap bone, is said in the play to have been a woman's: it may then stand for Isis, because she was the throne of Egypt on whose lap sat each of its rulers in turn; the ideogram of Isis' name is a throne. Perhaps a reader versed in numerology would understand by what coincidence the sums of blackmail money in *Chantaje* should be sixty and six hundred thousand dollars, while in *Dique seco*, the value of six million sestertia varies between sixty and one hundred and twenty million liras, and the marquess pays one hundred and twenty gold pieces for the falcon worth sixty pieces.

VII   *Meaning and Evaluation*

The three plays, *Soluna*, *Chantaje*, and *Dique seco*, contain numerous similarities, raising the question as to whether some organic relationship may exist between them. One general observation about them bears this out: the scenic antithesis of light and darkness, sound and silence, which all three (and even *Cuculcán*) have in common, are visual and auditory metaphors which express the inner polarity in our psychic nature. In Jung's conception this polarity underlies the dynamics of the psyche. Without it the psyche disintegrates, because any kind of onesidedness leads to pathological disturbances. The dynamic tension between the conscious and the unconscious, like all opposites, seeks to achieve and maintain a balance. Its movement alternates continuously from pole to pole. Ideally, the over-all direction of such movement carries the individual through the progressive stages of psychic development to Self-realization.[14]

For an example of the psychic effect of a onesided disorder we have, in *Dique seco*, Asturias' instruction to the stage manager to amplify throughout the theater the sound made by the jazz orchestra until actual distress is felt by the audience. This is another auditory metaphor. It is a way of illustrating the psychogenetic distress caused by a stagnation of energy at either pole. A balance between sound and silence may be harmonious, but a onesided excess is bound to produce disorder. The prevalence of neurosis symptomatic of our era is said to derive largely from our onesided overemphasis on rationalism and consciousness.

In addition to technical similarities, such as the use of light and sound, there is a thematic continuity that binds these plays and makes a trilogy of them. Together they outline the mythic and psychological stages of the development of personality, from beginning to end, from the uroboros to Self-realization. The four characters that make up the imaginary protagonist of this subdrama are: the blind violinist and Atchis, starring respectively in the creation and hero myths, the Marquess of Alconave in the transformation myth typified by Osiris, and lastly, Mauro in the stage where opposites are joined and the personality is finally consolidated—each phase overlapping somewhat with the others. The correct order of the plays is therefore not the chronological order in which they were written and as they were examined here, but as follows: *Chantaje, Dique seco, Soluna.* This is the order in which Asturias rearranged them when he gathered them together in one volume.

The theater of Asturias is above all poetic and fanciful, and we know from Surrealism and from psychology that fantasy and poetry are often more real than outward reality. As in the case of his novels, it is difficult to distinguish any single, decisive meaning for his plays or their symbols; various interpretations present themselves. This polivalence has the paradoxical result of actually making his theater *realistic*, but in a higher sense than the usual literary meaning of the word. It is the nature of psychic manifestations and experience to have more than one possible meaning; and it is usual for the unconscious to put forth equivocal symbols. Inasmuch as the plays are about processes occurring in the psyche, their ambiguity turns out to be intensely realistic; perhaps we might better say that they are super-realistic.

None of these three plays are closet dramas, however. On the contrary, they would be effective and pleasing spectacles. This is not surprising because Asturias' poetic gifts are essentially perceptive and he prefers to communicate experience as he receives it, through the senses. Even in his novels and tales he tends to stage his material, presenting it by means of intense visual images, through vibrant word harmony, and heightening its impact on the senses by devices normally reserved for poetry. He has known how to adapt this quality to stage requirements. There is an occasional lapse into fiction in *Dique seco*, where the novelist, not the dramatist, writes that the mariner hides the femur bone from Jemmy's sight "out of superstitious fear of the Negro's glance" (p. 80); but the play does not hang on these instructions, and they do elucidate the scene behind the literal scene. The author's novel use of light and sound has more than a decorative value; it forwards the action. The various dances, the byplay, the humorous mime, all contribute magnificent scenic entertainment. Furthermore, these highly theatrical plays have the virtue of addressing themselves directly to the spectators' unconscious. This is the reverse of dream procedure, whereby the unconscious tries to communicate with consciousness.

In this respect, I believe that Asturias' plays constitute an entirely new experiment in theater, although it may only be a return to something that is very old.[15] They do not emphasize plot or character in the customary sense. Their matter is chiefly psychological, not by means of conventional character analysis, but in the concealed manner that we have seen. In breaking new ground and applying to the stage the peculiar strategy he has used in fiction, Asturias may be laying the foundations for a new form of theater. It is difficult to foresee the extent of his influence or to judge how viable the theatrical form he gives to his concept will be. I have tried to visualize each play as a performance, and I think they would be entertaining and visually satisfying as they stand, especially *Dique seco* and *Soluna*. The additional levels of meaning they conceal would not, at this time, be immediately apparent to audiences, to say the least.[16] Nevertheless, it is conceivable and even likely that when the basic ideas of Jung become more widely known, there will evolve future audiences who can fully respond to this subtle twofold presentation.

Is there any way that the form of theater Asturias has created might be carried to greater perfection? The first answer that comes to mind is: yes, by making them more meaningful on the image level; in this respect the physical plot of *Soluna* best embodies the idea of the union of opposites that informs it. But such a judgment is based on the tenets of a traditional theater whose conventions have been shaken to the roots in the course of the last fifty years.

Besides, the ritually enacted myths which must have partly inspired the plays were themselves not noticeably profound; the story they told was often neither clear nor logically motivated in our modern sense, nor directly related to their purpose. Yet their psychological meaning was profound and it was effective. This was true even in spite of the participants; they did not have to understand the full meaning of what was going on in order to benefit from it, because the main action of the ritual unfolded wholly on the level of the unconscious. Furthermore, a relationship between the apparent and hidden meanings of the plays is sufficiently indicated by Asturias' technique, by his manner of presenting them: the unreality that modifies their superficial realism clearly informs us that we are in the presence of a suprasensible event that seems to bypass the barriers of rationalism and speak directly to the unconscious.

The historical drama, *La audiencia de los confines*, stands by itself. It is more static, less of a spectacle than the others, although sixteenth-century costumes and scenery could give it visual glamor. Being based on events and a situation drawn from history, most of the action takes place off stage; it begins necessarily with a conventional expository conversation, whereas the other plays begin *in media res*. Putting the latter three plays on the stage would require the imaginative audacity of an experimental art theater group. *La audiencia* demands the practical audacity of social reformers! The fact that until the Nobel Prize it was the only play of Asturias to have been staged reflects the public's preference for realistic theater and topical subjects although many additional factors militate against the production of any play at all in small Latin American countries.

La audiencia was probably chosen for its subject matter rather than for its author. This is fairly representative of the treatment Asturias has experienced in regard to his writings generally. The writer has been overshadowed by the immediacy of what he has had to say. Most of his critics and his public are understandably carried away by the questions he raises, and set out to demonstrate with historical and social references the accuracy of the conditions he describes. Those of his works which appear to have no social relevance are often brushed aside or totally ignored. Nevertheless, for all their urgency social issues are ultimately of secondary importance and can provide a satisfactory topic of literature only as a framework or in some other secondary function. It is conceivable that social disorders will change, whereas the nature and structure of the psyche, subjects which underlie the thinking of Asturias, do not. The influence of unconscious archetypes on human behavior, the basic myths which man endlessly relives, these are the fundamental themes that give meaning to his work.

CHAPTER 10

Short Stories

A STURIAS is an irrepressible storyteller, and we find many a tale integrated into his novels. For example, there is the story about two Indians who pool their resources to buy a big jug of liquor in order to retail it by the drink at a fiesta. They agree to split investment, labor, and profits down the line and to keep their sales on a strict cash basis: they themselves must pay if they want a drink. Early in the morning they depart for a distant village where they purchase the liquor and find that it costs six pesos less than expected. On the way back, the sun is high, the jug is heavy, so each one buys himself a three-peso drink with his leftover money. With the three pesos each one receives, each buys himself another shot, and again and again the money changes hands back and forth, while they begin to figure the profit they will net from all the sales. Before they ever make it back to the fiesta the jug is empty, and the police find them on the outskirts of town. One of the Indians is Goyo Yic, and it is this spree that lands him in the island prison. In the tradition of Mark Twain, the yarn rambles cheerily over ten pages as the speech of the two men thickens, and Goyo winds up conversing with María Tecún, or so he imagines.

Asturias plans to finish four more volumes of stories that he has not been able to fit into his novels, in addition to the three he has published to date. His first book, *Leyendas de Guatemala* (1930, Legends of Guatemala), and his most recent one, *El espejo de Lida Sal* (1967, Lida Sal's Looking Glass), have much in common; they are tales and legends, mostly Indian, some with a Spanish colonial background. *Leyendas*, dedicated to "my mother, who told me stories," contains the legends behind some still current beliefs, told in a prose of great enchantment which the poet Paul Valéry described as an elixir: "Reading it was like taking a philter, for this book is one to be imbibed rather than read."[1]

Valéry's simile is particularly descriptive of Asturias' Indian stories because they do have the effect of a magical potion. In them the author is able to create a wonderful suspension of time that makes us experience the undifferentiated attitude of Indians toward our categories of past, present, and future. The suspension of natural laws feels as normal in that world as it does in dreams. One of the loveliest tales is entitled "Leyenda de las Tablillas que Cantan" ("Legend of the Singing Tablets", referring to the tablets upon which poets inscribed their verses). It contains a statement on the creative process. An Indian poet of yore, Utuquel, is on his way to a week-long poetry contest held in one of the great Maya cities such as Tikal, of which only the marvelous ruins now remain: "To create is to steal, here, there, everywhere, on a big scale and on a small scale," he reflects, "to steal whatever is needed for the work of art. There is not and there cannot be a work by any one man, an original work. . . . All works of art belong to others, to those who lend them to us from deep inside ourselves. No matter how much we may say they are ours, they belong to the hidden echoes; yet, borrowed or stolen, we display them as our own while the century passes."[2]

Although these words can be understood literally, they allude to the psychology of artistic creation which surges from the collective unconscious, from the primordial archetypes we inherit with our human nature, common secrets and experiences hidden in the depths of our psyche that only the sensitivity of the artist can reveal to us. It is in this sense that Utuquel can say that his work proceeds from "deep inside ourselves," from the "hidden echoes," and that each age hears those echoes thanks to its respective poets. Jung has said as much,[3] and Asturias broached the subject once before in the conversation between Moncha and Hilario (*Hombres de maíz*). It would seem false and impertinent to inject a modern interpretation into a tale so eminently outside of time were it not that the collective treasure of the unconscious is the only authentic basis for universality that mankind commands—a universality that is beyond and independent of time and space.

I Week-end en Guatemala

Week-end en Guatemala (1956) belongs to Asturias' protest literature. It is a collection of stories focused on the invasion of Guatemala by Castillo Armas in 1954 which led to the fall of President Arbenz. The author moves around his subject viewing it from different moments in time and space, as a camera might. In eight fictional episodes he leads us from the situation as it was before the invasion on to an unspecified time in the future when the calamities of the invasion will be rectified, portraying the attitudes of the principal social groups involved: army, landlords, students, laborers, Indians.

In some editions the stories are captioned chapters, which has led to the book's being considered a novel. But other than a common historical focus, there is no link between the eight stories; the characters and situation of each one are different. The plots tend to be loosely constructed, (all but one, "Toro-tumbo"). The resulting succession of vivid, shocking scenes produces an over-all effect of tessellation; the reader may not remember the connection between incidents, but the total picture is clear: in order to retain their privileges, the feudal classes enlist the assistance of the United States to re-establish a dictatorship and oust the beneficiaries of land reforms; they do this in the name of anti-communism.

This is the book in which Asturias unburdens himself of the outrage he and many of his compatriots felt over the American intervention in Guatemala, for without it the invasion would not have succeeded. For him personally, the downfall of the revolutionary government, which had lasted from 1944 to 1954, was perhaps a more bitter disappointment than for others. Retaining the idealism of his student days, he had devoted himself to writing, teaching, fighting, and pleading for justice toward the Indians and the poor of his country. This was the first regime to share his concern. In 1952 a program of agrarian reform was inaugurated, and Indians began to receive parcels of land which had been held idle by large landowners. Writing that year from Bolivia, where similar conditions prevailed, Asturias joyously described himself as a writer from "one of the freest countries in America, Guatemala."[4] We know from his trilogy how he felt about the social revolution of 1944 and about the freely elected governments that followed: it was under these administrations that he first entered the diplomatic corps. Besides, he had never before been free to publish his first novel, and it is only since then that he has written the bulk of his work. As ambassador to El Salvador Asturias prevented Castillo Armas from invading Guatemala over that border. In retaliation, the Colonel deprived him of his citizenship as soon as he came to power. No wonder each bomb dropped on Guatemalan soil by American planes exploded in his blood.[5]

In *Week-end* Asturias has struck every note in his emotional repertoire, from understatement to overstatement. One of the most forceful tales, because of its muted tones, is the five-page "El Bueyón" ("The Big Ox"), about a peasant woman who had never seen a plane, much less a bomb, and who lives through the horror of having her husband disappear from before her eyes in what seems to be a ghastly piece of magic. Most of the stories are a mixture of pathos, farce, and grisly satire, reflecting the horror and grotesque disproportion between the various factions. The new weapons, public relations and propaganda, have their vital roles. Nothing can begin until a publicity campaign has had time to prepare world opinion, and as soon as the coup is accomplished another huge campaign must be waged through the news media to justify it. In a course on advertising taken by a Guatemalan student in an American university, the professor explains that the aim of advertising is to convert a slogan into a sign that will release a reflex action. The secret is to find the key word that will penetrate into the mind of millions of people without their reflecting on its meaning, so that they will react to what the word represents rather than to what it means. In the case of Guatemala the key word is communism. Massive advertising has emptied the word of its ideological meaning and converted it into a danger signal: danger signals are accepted at face value: nobody tests the veracity of a skull-and-crossbones sign on a bottle. The danger is created by the sign. Thus, by applying the word "communism" to a country of three million people, which could never threaten United States security, let alone the world's, Guatemala is converted into a danger. Advertising, the professor concludes, is ideographic; good advertisers think signs, not ideas.

II *"Torotumbo"*

The last story of the collection, "Torotumbo," is in a sense extraneous to the invasion cycle and, unlike the others, it is entirely intelligible without preknowledge of political circumstances. It is laid at some hypothetical time when dictatorship shall be put down by the concerted movement of the people—an echo of *Los ojos de los enterrados*. The movement of events throughout its forty pages is set off by what happens in the first three, giving the line of action a unity and coherence that make it the best story of the lot in the conventional sense, and one of the best Asturias has written.

A little girl of seven strays into the storerooms of a purveyor of masquerade costumes while her father and godfather, two rustic Indians from the mountains, are renting the accoutrements for a religious fiesta. She comes across the great red mask and costume of a devil; frightened, she suddenly discovers that she is lost and begins to scream. But the two men have left the store, thinking she is outside, and only the storekeeper, Tamagas, hears her. When he comes hurrying up, he looks just as frightful as the devil, and when he starts kissing and biting her hands and ears, she feels sure he is about to eat her. In fact, he rapes her, and when he has finished he sees that she is dead.

A knocking at the front tells him that the child's parents are back. Covering her body with the red devil, he climbs out the back, circles around the block, and comes innocently down the street toward the waiting men. He lets them in, and when they find her body under the devil, he convinces them that it was the devil, incarnate in the red costume, who did the deed. They leave with the little corpse, credulous and even grateful to Tamagas for not reporting them to the police.

But Tamagas has not been as lucky as he thinks. He belongs to the Committee of Defense Against Communism, a group of zealots who encourage anonymous denunciations of Communist suspects and turn over the names to the police. When the little girl screamed, a neighbor heard her, jumped over the garden wall, and saw what happened. He is Tizonelli, an Italian vegetable man, an anarchist and a loner, whose hobby is to contravene the dictatorship in every way he can. To pay for his silence, Tamagas, whose name is that of a poisonous snake, must provide Tizonelli, whose name contains the word firebrand, with the daily list of suspects the committee gives to the police.

The story is laid in the future, but we are back in the atmosphere of *El Señor Presidente* except that by now priests have become active supporters of the oppression, and the oppression is dignified with the name of anti-communism. Padre Berenice is the head of the local committee, although the supreme head is an American who wears a hood, after the fashion of Klansmen. The committee members soon begin to look upon one another with suspicion, because thanks to Tizonelli all their suspects disappear before they can be apprehended. Tamagas' conscience bothers him. He decides to confess everything to Padre Berenice but at the last moment he loses courage and merely tells the story as the Indians believed it: that a little girl was violated by a red devil in the back of his store.

To the padre the "event" is highly portentous. It is a case of incubus which he interprets as follows: the red devil is communism; the defenseless child represents Guatemala, violated and bloodied by Communist subversion. He proposes that the desecration be cleansed by an auto-da-fé held on the spot where it occurred, in Tamagas' house. There, in the presence of church and state dignitaries, the incarnation of communism, the red devil, shall be officially delivered to the flames. Tamagas is not enthusiastic about having his red devil burned and confides the plan to Tizonelli. When the Italian hears that the president, the archbishop, the nuncio, and the committee officials will gather in the costume shop, he immediately arranges to insert dynamite into the devil's headdress so that it will explode when thrown into the fire.

Meanwhile the two Indians have gone home with the child. Besides her obsequies, they have the urgent duty of performing the Torotumbo dance, because in the case of a devil violating a maiden, it must be danced to prevent drought and other agricultural calamities. Starting from the child's village, the hypnotic cadence of the dance beats over the countryside; ever more and more dancers surrender to the frenzy of the rhythm and apply themselves to translating into motion the religious import of their animal masks and costumes. The symbolism of the bull predominates, as the name *Toro*tumbo indicates. The dancers advance toward the city and the suburban populace sallies forth to receive them. It might have ended there, except that students heard about the Torotumbo and wanted to bring the cortege into town for an off-season carnival.

On the day of the auto-da-fé, the Torotumbo is at its height. Tizonelli is hovering around the store to see the dignitaries arrive when a group of merrymakers drag him away—in fun, he thinks at first, but as they whisk him into a car and out beyond the city, he learns that they are some of the revolutionaries he has saved from the police. They know about the auto-da-fé, and they want Tizonelli to help them capture the president and other officials. Capture them? Pick up their pieces, more likely! The Italian reveals his dynamite prowess and is chagrined at their reaction: the infernal machine must be dismounted immediately because their revolution, scheduled to begin today, does not allow for violence. What kind of chivalrous rebels are these? wonders Tizonelli. Are they planning a sportsmanlike revolution? Still clad as merrymakers, the men jump into the car with Tizonelli and speed back to the capital, but alas the Torotumbo has taken over the city and the streets are impassable.

The last six pages are a nightmarish attempt to reach the house of Tamagas, inching through the dancing mobs. In these pages the author slows down the tempo and portrays the suspense and anxiety of interminable time, rendering the feel of duration as the characters experience it. Eventually the explosion does occur, and Tizonelli learns that the revolutionaries' takeover in another part of the city is successful. The story ends as the participants of the Torotumbo surge out of the city and up the mountain slopes with the light of a new day in their eyes.

Castelpoggi, the Argentine critic, sees this story as a great allegory about an insurgence against oppression, presented under the appearance of a ritual dance. The Italian writer Bellini interprets it to mean that dictatorship will fall definitively when people rediscover their ties with the past.[6] Assuming that "ties with the past" refers to the Torotumbo, both critics are correct, but neither explains just how the dance is linked with the overthrow of the dictator. In the text the Torotumbo is the cover under which the revolutionaries carry out their coup, but the Indians themselves have no political intentions.

At the risk of being overexplicit, I would like to supply the details because the link does not seem obvious to me. The Torotumbo is basically a fertility dance: the name could be informally translated as "bull hop" and has obvious fertility connotations; besides, the purpose of the dance is to prevent a drought—the drought that would have followed the violation of a maiden by a devil. This takes us back to one of the themes of *El Señor Presidente* where dictatorship was equated with sterility and death. If the little Indian girl represents Guatemala, the devil (or Tamagas) who violated her, represents the dictatorship; and the Torotumbo, danced to avert the effect of dictatorship on Guatemala, stands for the communal action of the people against the destruction wrought by tyranny. The Indians' instinctive, unerring recognition of whatever operates against the vital principle and their spontaneous rejection of it, are expressed in mythic and ritualistic form, here, in the Torotumbo. These are the roots and "ties with the past" that the people as a whole must recover if they are to attain decisive freedom. The knowledge that primitive men have retained has slipped away from civilized men due to their overreliance on the intellect.

In the story, the privileged classes remain aloof from the people; they celebrate the fiesta in their private patios, dance other dances than the Torotumbo, or watch the populace from balconies. In contrast, the revolutionaries join the dancers, don their costumes, and make themselves one with the participants of the ritual. Thus, under the aegis of the Torotumbo, they carry out on a conscious plane that which the dancers are effecting on the level of myth: they are insuring the land against drought and sterility.

Once again Asturias demonstrates the psychic truth of myth and the urgent need modern man has for wholeness, which is to say, a balance between spirit and matter, between reason and instinct, a return to the "roots" of the unconscious which primitive man has preserved.

Epilogue

The last three novels of Asturias are replete with suggestive material that invites further study, but space limitations do not allow for it here.

El alhajadito, 1961 (The Little Bejeweled One), bears little resemblance to his other writings. It is divided into three episodes. The first concerns the daydreams of a boy who imagines himself to be the last descendant of a family called los Alhajados, men who wore black clothes and jewels, who never died but simply disappeared. As lord of the land, he allows an imaginary circus to set up on his property and partakes of their intrigues. The second episode, told in the first person plural, is about the pursuit of a phantom ship by pursuers who themselves seem to be phantasms. The elusive beauty of these sixteen pages place them among the loveliest pieces Asturias has written. The third episode, told in the first person by the same child, reveals that he is the bastard son of two poverty-stricken sisters; he never learns which is his mother.

The Guatemalan version of the Faust legend tells that in exchange for riches a man sells his *wife* to the devil, instead of his soul, which is not so different anyway, in Jungian terms. Asturias offers an enactment of this legend as a starter for the remarkable adventures told in *Mulata de tal* (1963). Yumí, an Indian peasant, sells his wife Catalina to Tazol, the devil of corn husks (i.e., detritus) who carries her off in a gust of wind. To match his new riches Yumí acquires a new, seductive wife, the Mulata; but, carrying out the legend, he receives his punishment from that which he coveted. The new wife proves to be asexual, ferocious and destructive. Without looking very hard one can recognize in her the characteristics of the negative anima. As a parable of the modern world, the legend

161

shows that man, in an excess of ambition and avarice, has forsaken his link with the unconscious while reaching for the treasures of technology and scientific advances—but the unconscious returns to torment him in its negative aspect by luring him to destruction. Here the negative anima takes the form of a *femme fatale*, the fascinating Mulata. Fortunately, Yumí's psychic health is better than the average Western man's; he has the good sense to get back his good wife, and she helps him get rid of the Mulata for a while.

The legend takes up about forty pages, and from there we follow Yumí and his wife into a world of prodigies, sorcery, giants, and other fabulous creatures, where the author gives rein to the "prose of fire" cited by the Swedish Academy when it awarded him the Nobel Prize.

It is important to realize that the magic and fantastic elements in this and other books, such as dead animals that rise up and speak, women who change into dwarfs, or men into their nahual animals, are no more than the portrayal of things as his characters see them. Asturias explains that the people, Indian and mestizo, defend themselves from the long persecution to which they have been subjected by recourse to the world that lies beyond the visible, that of magic reality. Because this world is so real to them and because Central America, with its paradisiac but capricious nature, is innately superrealistic, his characters live comfortably in a zone where, as he says, dreams are transformed into tangible and visible forms.

Maladrón 1969 (Bad Thief), laid in sixteenth-century Guatemala, is about a group of Spanish soldiers ("turtle men" to the Indians on account of their armor) who are looking for a water route between the two oceans. The title derives from the cult promoted by some of them to the Bad Thief of the Crucifixion, who, they say, was in reality a scholarly Sadducee. He had laughed at Christ on the cross because he did not believe in the immortality of the soul, nor in the resurrection of the dead, nor in retribution. The materialistic creed of his followers is considered suitable and appealing to the rough and tough mentality of the conquistadors; Christianity could promise no more than an eternity of hell to them who brought hell on earth wherever they went. No comfort for them in believing in another life, and much in denying it! The novel also deals with the Indians and offers a splendid evocation of the mentality of both groups.

A lesser known aspect of Asturias is his career as a newspaperman. Ever since the 1920's when he went to live in Europe, Latin American journals have been featuring his articles on their editorial pages. He began by sending back accounts of his experiences, such as interviews with Unamuno and Blasco Ibáñez, and now, nearly fifty years later, one still finds his essays in current dailies. Many of these writings are on literary subjects: reminiscences of old friends and tributes to admired colleagues such as Gabriela Mistral, whose concern for American Indians endeared her to him as far back as his student days; Barba Jacob, Gertrude Stein, Rafael Alberti and Rubén Darío, whom he met in Guatemala shortly before his death in 1916, and who may well be the poet in *El Señor Presidente*. One recent article of Asturias protested the widespread commercial exploitation of García Lorca that disseminates the false image of the Spanish poet as an irresponsible child or "gypsy," noting that there are many who play down the fact of his assassination, despising his sacrifice and attempting to sever his bond with the common people, with whom Lorca had chosen to side against the forces that oppress them.

Many others of Asturias' articles are familiar essays in the best discursive tradition of writing as process, certainly a departure from the customary intention of his prose. With the charm of a Pied Piper he draws us into the recesses of his mind. Starting from a given subject, say, mobile sculptures, he guides us through the thoughts that crowd up to him, lightly touching on some as he moves along; he suggests the idea of perpetual motion as adventure that restores the vitality of childhood to us; he comments on the mobile's gratuitous movement in a utilitarian world; on animation without rhyme or reason that breathes magic and a secret life into our homes, whether we be there or not; on mobiles as toys that help us struggle against death, the immutable; and he does not forget the classic digression, one about some sheets of writing paper slipping from his desk to become mobiles in their own right as he chases them

over the carpet. These informal essays are particularly precious
for the insight they afford into a more personal side of the
author. Except for an eighty-page booklet containing fourteen
of them, his articles have not yet been collected and made
readily available, which leaves a big lacuna in our knowledge of
the Asturian opus.

Like Dickens, Asturias possesses a boundless gift of characterization. He has the ability to seize upon the essential traits
and penetrate into the consciousness of a vast range of individuals in the composite of Guatemalan society. Vices, foibles,
and unconscious virtues are dramatized, the zeal of youth,
the perceptions of simple folk. Sabina, the unlettered house-
keeper of *El papa verde*, like Moncha of *Hombres de maíz*,
is one whose ponderings over the mysteries of life reflect
the ingenuous sagacity of her kind. Unlike Dickens, Asturias
does not use catch phrases or mannerisms to define his
characters, but rather their outlook on life, in keeping with his
avowed purpose of giving voice to the common people and
to their aspirations. Even the nature of certain animals is
portrayed, and some are endowed with a role and personality:
who could forget Jazmín, the skinny little dog of Nicho, or
Juper, the huge, frisky hound that Juambo looked after? If
ever the nations of Latin America develop a novel-reading
public comparable to that of England, the characters of Asturias are sure to live as vividly in popular culture as those of
the English writer.

One of the great successes of Asturias is to have captured
and reproduced the mind of the Indians, their view of the
world, and their experience of it. He shares this virtue with his
former Sorbonne professor, Georges Raynaud. Instead of minimizing the oddities and reducing the Indian texts to European
terms to make them intelligible, Raynaud preferred to adjust
his own mind and language to fit their thought patterns and
to preserve their original essence. This makes his translations
more accurate but more difficult to read than if he had used
the reductive method. Asturias seems to use the same principle
as Raynaud: in many of his Indian legends and in a novel like
Mulata, he makes little or no concession to the Western turn

of mind. Instead, he conveys his insight into the native mentality as it is, and offers us an opportunity to penetrate into this world of unreal reality insofar as we are willing to make the effort to follow him. One's natural tendency is to translate the unfamiliar into known terms and to disregard what cannot be so handled. But the readers of Asturias owe it to him to throw off the moorings of Western culture and allow themselves to be submerged in the unfamiliar and mysterious life he has re-created. Then one begins to experience how the world looks to a Maya Indian. It is said that Asturias is fond of automatic writing; perhaps by submitting to his guidance along this course, we will perceive the chords he stirs in our unconscious and respond sympathetically to the spirit of this ancient people.

There is a running debate among Latin Americans over two trends in their literature; the majority feel that as artists they are committed to portraying the conditions existing in their country; the others argue that only universal themes are worthy of treatment, and that the use of political and social topics will prevent the fiction of this continent from ever reaching the stature of European literature—as if there were an unbreachable gap between the two stands. Adherents of this group reject thesis literature, forgetting that a piece of fiction ceases to be propaganda when the characters and situations are true and the art of the novelist gives them life. Asturias, also, rejects the "billboard novel," as he puts it, but he stands squarely in the main stream of thesis literature, regarding the combative novel as being most suited to the times. Philosophic questing, existential introspection, and other European imports that preoccupy intellectual minorities over here, seem to him luxuries that are not wholly relevant in a continent still so far from achieving the minimum requisites for human living.

The real difference between the two literary groups, it seems to me, is that the advocates of universal topics consider Latin American literature to be part of European literature, whereas the others think that it is and should be something different. At least, this is Asturias' opinion. As we know, he has pointed out that ever since the beginning, writers in

Latin America have possessed certain distinctive characteristics: an attitude of protest against the continual exploitation
of this continent and its people; an attentiveness to nature,
its forces, first fruits, animals, climate, and the bearing of
these elements on American life; and recently an awareness
that in order to express the peculiar quality of American
reality, a new poetic idiom had to be forged. His goal has been
to establish for the New World new frames of reference, not in
contempt for those of the Old World, but to give expression to
the authentic American ethos that continues to thrive and
develop without fitting into the molds of any other culture.

Now, given the close attention Asturias has devoted to the
American scene, and given his reputation as a social and
political protester, can it be said that his writings exclude
universal themes? We have seen that they are far from doing
so. Within a framework of social reality or of Indian folklore
he has treated universal truths, combining these spheres of
interest in an original and surprising manner. Transcending
philosophical fashions, he has linked his created universe with
the dawn of history and his twentieth-century characters with
myths from all cultures, and thereby demonstrated the immutability of human nature across the world and through the
ages. He has accomplished this, not by running two kinds of
meaning along parallel lines, but by showing the relationship
between them. In other words, he has projected the temporal
against the eternal, the local against the universal, and shown
the timeless aspect of man's needs.

Notes and References

Chapter One

1. Miguel Angel Asturias, *La arquitectura de la vida nueva* (Guatemala, 1928), pp. 17, 20.

2. Based on Miguel Angel Asturias, "Originalità e caratteristiche del romanzo latino-americano," *Terzo programma: quaderni trimestrali* No. 4. (Turin, 1964), pp. 51–74, and interviews.

Chapter Two

1. Luis Alberto Sánchez, *La tierra del quetzal* (Santiago de Chile, 1950), p. 189.

2. Ricardo Navas Ruíz, "Tiempo y palabra en Miguel Angel Asturias," *Quaderni Iberoamericani* (December 1963), pp. 276–82.

3. Miguel Angel Asturias, *El Señor Presidente* (Buenos Aires, 1959), p. 276. Subsequent page numbers will refer to this edition.

4. This scene seems to be an hallucination which would be psychologically justified in view of Don Miguel's deep involvement in the fertility-destruction conflict. Nevertheless, the dictator Estrada Cabrera (1898–1920), on whom this President is modeled, did surround himself with Indian sorcerers.

5. Considerations of emphasis lead us to presume that little Miguel was conceived on this occasion.

6. To the objection that Miguel never knew he had a son, it is answered that the fertility-destruction conflict occurs on the unconscious level; Miguel and the President represent blind forces. By destroying Miguel while unwittingly allowing him to communicate life, the President imitates Nature which is ruthless to the individual but careful of the species.

Chapter Three

1. "Homenaje a Miguel Angel Asturias," *Repertorio Americano* (San José, Costa Rica, March 1, 1950), p. 83; Luis Harss, *Into the Mainstream: Conversations with Latin-American Writers* (New York, 1967), p. 79.

2. By baroque requirements I mean the necessity in which the American writer has always been of providing his European reader with detailed descriptions of the unfamiliar objects of this continent, as the Cuban novelist Alejo Carpentier explains in *Tientos y diferencias* (Mexico, 1964), pp. 40–43.

3. The Maya have their own fertility and rebirth myth, told in the *Popol Vuh* and equal in beauty to any. The fullest interpretation of the myth is found in the work of anthropologist Rafael Girard; as it is not readily available, the following synopsis is included: The essential function of a fertility god is to go underground or to die and be buried like a seed, in order to be reborn and to bear fruit. Thus, the Maya-Quiché fertility god, Hun-Hunahpú, receives an invitation to the underworld, Xibalba, where he is overpowered and beheaded by the Lords of Death. His head is hung on a calabash tree where it becomes indistinguishable from the fruit. A maiden of Xibalba, Xquic (pronounced Ishkik) comes to admire the fruit and is about to pluck it when the head of Hun-Hunahpú addresses her asking her to stretch forth her hand. She does, whereupon he lets his spittle fall on her open palm and she conceives his progeny. He directs her to the upperworld and, although she is a child of Death, he promises her life if she will believe his word. She finds her way out of Xibalba and to the house of his mother, Xmucané, where she gives birth to twins: Hunahpú and Xbalanqué. In this way the fertility god is reborn in his children. Hunahpú is the young corn and culture god. He establishes the ritual whereby the sacred food, corn, shall be planted and cultivated. Then with his sister Xbalanqué, he departs for the underworld. In the course of defeating the Lords of Death who had killed his father, he and his sister die voluntarily knowing they are to be reborn on the fifth day, just as corn planted in the hot lowlands where the Maya originated sprouts on the fifth day. After further adventures, the twins rise into the heavens where Hunahpú becomes the sun and Xbalanqué, the moon. Ultimately there are only two Maya gods, Sun and Moon; each have three epiphanies (which in turn have several manifestations): the grandfather Sun, supreme god; the Father or Fertility god, often represented as a reptile, known as God B in Yucatan; and the son, the young and beautiful corn god, comparable to Adonis except that he is also the Sun, which Adonis is not. Likewise, Xbalanqué is the young crescent Moon; her mother, Xquic, is the full Moon, and the old Moon is the Grandmother, Xmucané; Moon is also the Goddess of Rain, and the phases of the moon, seen as a jug, are graphic evidence of her store of water.

4. Representations of Ishtar sometimes show her holding a ring which is said to refer to her control over the continuity of life.

5. Erich Neumann, *The Great Mother: An Analysis of the Archetype*, trans. Ralph Manheim, Bollingen Series XLVII (New York, 1955), pls. 122–37.

6. Neumann, *Great Mother*, pls. 24, 49.

7. H. W. F. Saggs, *The Greatness That Was Babylon: A Sketch of the Ancient Civilization of the Tigris-Euphrates Valley* (New York, 1962), p. 486.

8. André Parrot, *Babylon and the Old Testament*, trans. B. E. Hooke, "Studies in Biblical Archeology" No. 8 (New York, 1958), pp. 76, 149; Ezekiel 8:16–17.

9. Neumann, *Great Mother*, p. 216.

10. The Royal Tombs of Ur were discovered by Sir Leonard Woolley in the 1920's while the novel was being written. At Ur when the king died, his consort and his whole retinue lay down in adjacent tombs and were buried with him, presumably after taking poison. Sumeria, bordering on and older than Babylonia, is thought to have been the birthplace of the Ishtar myths. Incidentally, the obscene drawings on the walls of Fedina's cell are phallic symbols while others, such as boats, cradles, bottles, eyes, moons, mermaids, circles, and guitars, all have maternal connotations symbolizing the return to the womb or unconscious; number 13 is a kabalistic sign of death and rebirth. Similar meanings are apparent in the figures that Miguel scratched on his prison wall.

11. As seen in Chapter 2, the moment when Camila first reciprocates Miguel's love climaxes his metaphysical transformation.

12. Franz Cumont, *The Oriental Religions in Roman Paganism* (New York, 1956), pp. 170, 179.

13. Minor examples: Tícher with his mother, the brothel madam when she was the President's mistress, Juan Canales and his wife, Doctor Barreño and his better half.

14. At the other end of life, after maturation, the circle represents the Self, but this is a different matter. See, Erich Neumann, *The Origins and History of Consciousness*, trans. R. F. C. Hull, Bollingen Series XLII (New York, 1954), pp. 10, 416.

15. "A estas palabras sobrevino un ruido quisquilloso de reptil en tinieblas. . . . A partir de ese momento el prisionero empezó a rascarse como si le comiera el cuerpo que ya no sentía . . ." (p. 296).

16. From a talk given in Milan, 1964. Quoted by Giuseppe Bellini, *La narrativa di Miguel Ángel Asturias* (Milan, 1966), p. 36.

17. "Wotan," *Civilization in Transition* in *Collected Works*, 10 (New York, 1964).

18. Neumann, *Great Mother*, p. 196.

19. C. G. Jung, *Symbols of Transformation* in *Collected Works*, 5 (New York, 1956), p. 216.

Chapter Four

1. Substantiation for the foregoing is found in the following: Fernando Alegría, *Breve historia de la novela hispanoamericana* (Mexico, 1959), p. 225; Luis Harss and Barbara Dohmann, *Into the Mainstream: Conversations with Latin-American Writers* (New York, 1967), pp. 80, 87; Luis Alberto Sánchez, *La tierra del quetzal* (Santiago de Chile, 1950), p. 188; Enrique Anderson Imbert, *Historia de la literatura hispanoamericana* (Mexico, 1964), II, p. 226.

2. According to the anthropological research of Rafael Girard, *Los chortís ante el problema maya* (Mexico, 1958), the Maya corn myth told in the *Popol Vuh* constitutes one of the best integrated and most satisfying myths in the world. The worship and cultivation of corn, which is one and the same thing, regulates the leisure and occupations of the Indian, converting his labor into the holy and creative function of assisting the god of fertility, who is a homologue of the supreme god, the sun.

3. Miguel Angel Asturias, *Hombres de maíz* (Buenos Aires, 1957), p. 91. Subsequent page references will be to this edition.

4. The archetype that the two old men represent is that of the wise old man which is described in the chapter on *Viento fuerte*. The principal characteristic of the wise old man is to give advice, as did the one Nicho saw at Moncha's. Nicho "heard" Moncha speak to this man, but there is no indication that Moncha or anyone else saw him.

5. "La fondera... no le quitaba los ojos al relumbre *sangroso* del chal, más *vivo* cuando le pegaban los rayos del sol.... El chal corinto... ya no le parecía lindo sino *divino*" (pp. 152, 154).

6. "¡Caramba, no todo el tiempo es de jocotes!" p. 152). *Jocote* is a Guatemalan fruit like a plum.

7. Mircea Eliade, *Comos and History: The Myth of the Eternal Return* (New York, 1954), pp. 44–46.

Chapter Five

1. C. G. Jung, *Symbols of Transformation* in *Collected Works*, 5 (New York, 1956), pp. 431ff.

2. Jolande Jacobi, *The Way of Individuation* (New York, 1967), p. 68; Joseph Henderson and Maud Oakes, *The Wisdom of the Serpent: Myths of Death, Rebirth and Resurrection* (New York, 1963), ch. 5.

3. Erich Neumann, *The Origins and History of Consciousness* (New York, 1954). pp. 397–407.

4. C. G. Jung, *The Development of Personality* in *Collected Works*, 17 (New York, 1954), p. 199.

5. Jung, *Symbols of Transformation*, pp. 424, 432. He develops the meaning of and need for sacrifice, pp. 423–44. In modern man's disregard of the unconscious, Jungians see the principal danger that besets him: to cut off that source of life forces is an invitation to neuroses and other disorders.

6. "Aquí la mujer/yo el dormido" (p. 7). Asturias appears to have taken these words from an Aztec liturgical poem, "Canto a Atamalcualoyan."

Chapter Six

1. Miguel Angel Asturias, *Viento fuerte* (Buenos Aires, 1955), pp. 28–29. All page references in this chapter will be to this edition. Although quotation marks are used to indicate dialogue, this and other conversations are not necessarily word-for-word translations of Asturias' text, but, when appropriate, they only summarize the gist of the passage.

2. C. G. Jung, *The Archetypes and the Collective Unconscious* in *Collected Works*, 9 (New York, 1959), I, pp. 24–32, 184.

3. The Spanish dancer is compared to Dulcinea del Toboso, the imaginary lady who inspired Don Quixote—in other words, his anima. But the text of the novel says that the dancer is *not* Mead's Dulcinea. No. She is the negative aspect of his anima, whereas Dulcinea was a positive force for the don.

4. See note 3, Chapter 3.

5. Jung, *The Archetypes*, pp.31–33, 207–54.

6. In *Hombres de maíz*, the wise old man archetype for Nicho was first the (probably imaginary) man who led him to the cave, and later the (wholly imaginary) sorcerer inside the cave who looked just like him, both being projected extensions of his little dog (see Chapter 4, note 4 above).

7. C. D. Kepner, Jr. and J. H. Soothill, *The Banana Empire: A Case Study in Economic Imperialism* (New York, 1935).

8. *Atlas*, December 1967, pp. 56–57.

9. Harss, *Into the Mainstream*, p. 90.

Chapter Seven

1. In this novel the name Green Pope belongs exclusively to Geo Maker Thompson and is not applied to just any president of the fruit company as it was in *Viento fuerte;* the nameless company president

whom Lester Mead visited and referred to as the Green Pope was not Thompson, because Thompson became president after Mead's death. Asturias is frequently forgetful or inconsistent about small matters, especially in the trilogy, although the possibility that on another level he may have a reason for this must not be overlooked. It will be convenient to refer to Geo Maker Thompson henceforth as GMT, although Asturias does not; he calls him Maker Thompson, generally.

2. Miguel Angel Asturias, *El papa verde* (Buenos Aires, 1957), p. 228. Subsequent page numbers will refer to this edition.

Chapter Eight

1. The legend of Nanahuatl. Raynaud describes it in his version of the *Popol Vuh*, note 27 in "Vocabulario."

2. *Atlas*, December 1967, pp. 56–57.

Chapter Nine

1. C. G. Jung has explained the psychology of ritual dance: "The regression of the libido makes the ritual act of treading out the dance-step seem like the repetition of the infantile 'kicking.' The latter is associated with the mother and with pleasurable sensations. . . . The rhythm of the dance transports the dancer into an unconscious state." *Symbols of Transformation* in *Collected Works*, 5 (New York, 1956), p. 315.

2. Rafael Girard, *Esoterismo del Popol Vuh* (Mexico, 1948), pp. 253–80; also to be found in *Los Chortís ante el problema maya*, 5 vols. (Mexico, 1949), Vol. IV. Dr. Girard reports this material for the evidence it bears on his theory on the origin and development of the Mayas.

3. Harss, *Into the Mainstream*, p. 85.

4. Carlos Solórzano, ed., *Teatro guatemalteco contemporáneo* (Madrid, 1964), p. 21.

5. Miguel Angel Asturias, *Teatro: Chantaje, Dique seco, Soluna, La audiencia de los confines* (Buenos Aires, 1964), p. 168. All page numbers for these four plays refer to this edition. It is not clear to me why an eclipse of the moon, which takes place at night, is understood to be a struggle with the *sun*, unless the shadow of the earth is seen as a negative sun.

6. Jung, *Symbols of Transformation*, pp. 431–32.

7. Jolande Jacobi, *The Psychology of C. G. Jung* (New Haven 1962), pp. 106ff., 123.

8. Data on Las Casas obtained from Lewis Hanke, *The Spanish Struggle for Justice in the Conquest of America* (Philadelphia, 1949).

9. *Insula*, April 1963, p. 12.

10. Jung, *Memories, Dreams, Reflections* (New York, 1965), p. 256.

11. Erich Neumann, *The Origins and History of Consciousness*, trans. R. F. C. Hull, Bollingen Series XLII (New York, 1954), pp. 52ff.

12. In the 1920's Asturias wrote a short story laid in Paris, but he has not included it in any of his books. A French translation entitled "La barbe provisoire" may be read in *Les temps modernes*, No. 107, November 1954, pp. 637–49.

13. Neumann, *Origins*, p. 249.

14. Jacobi, *Psychology of C. G. Jung*, pp. 51ff.

15. Ionesco's *Victims of Duty* bears a slight resemblance to Asturias' plays insofar as the characters re-enact an archetypal struggle of the hero against his parents, but Ionesco handles the subject more overtly.

16. For example, it has not been generally noticed that in his film *Les Dimanches et Cybèle* (Sundays and Cybele), Serge Bourguignon has told the myth of Attis and Cybele in a subtle manner, similar to that used by Asturias. (See my note to *México en la cultura*, Feb. 7, 1965, p. 4: "Símbolos Secretos de una Bella Película.") Ingmar Bergman appears to have used an understructure of Great Mother mythology for Jungian purposes in films such as *Persona*.

Chapter Ten

1. Miguel Angel Asturias, *Leyendas de Guatemala* (Buenos Aires, 1957), pp. 7, 10.

2. Miguel Angel Asturias, *El espejo de Lida Sal* (Mexico, 1967), pp. 94–95.

3. C. G. Jung, "Psychology and Literature," *The Spirit in Man, Art and Literature* in *Collected Works*, 15 (New York, 1966).

4. Miguel Angel Asturias, *Carta aérea a mis amigos de América* (Buenos Aires, 1952), p. 7; a twelve-page pamphlet, no publisher.

5. For a commentary on United States intervention see Philip B. Taylor, Jr., "The Guatemalan Affair: A Critique of US Foreign Policy," *American Political Science Review*, L (September, 1956), pp. 787–806; David Wise and Thomas B. Ross, *The Invisible Government* (New York, 1964).

6. Atilio Jorge Castelpoggi, *Miguel Angel Asturias* (Buenos Aires, 1961), pp. 172–73; Giuseppe Bellini, *La narrativa di Miguel Angel Asturias* (Milan, 1966), p. 154.

Selected Bibliography

PRIMARY SOURCES

Los dioses, los héroes y los hombres de Guatemala antigua o el Libro del Consejo. Popol Vuh de los indios quichés. Tr. by Miguel Angel Asturias and J. Manuel González de Mendoza. Paris: 1927.

Anales de los Xahil de los indios cakchiqueles. Tr. by Miguel Angel Asturias and J. Manuel González de Mendoza. Paris: 1928.

La arquitectura de la vida nueva. Guatemala: Goubaud, 1928.

Leyendas de Guatemala. Madrid: Oriente, 1930.

El Señor Presidente. Mexico: Costa-Amic, 1946 (privately published). Buenos Aires: Losada, 1948. *El Señor Presidente* (in English). Tr. by Frances Partridge. London: Victor Gollancz, 1963 and New York: Atheneum, 1964.

Sien de alondra (preface by Alfonso Reyes). Buenos Aires: Argos, 1949.

Hombres de maíz. Buenos Aires: Losada, 1949.

Viento fuerte. Buenos Aires: Losada, 1950. *Strong Wind.* Tr. Gregory Rabassa. Boston: Delacorte, 1969.

El papa verde. Buenos Aires: Losada, 1954.

Soluna. Buenos Aires: Losange, 1955.

Week-end en Guatemala. Buenos Aires: Goyanarte, 1956.

La audiencia de los confines. Buenos Aires: Ariadna, 1957.

Nekrasof. Tr. by Miguel Angel Asturias in *Teatro: J. P. Sartre.* Buenos Aires: Losada, 1957.

Los ojos de los enterrados. Buenos Aires: Losada, 1960.

Poesía precolombina. Ed. by Miguel Angel Asturias. Buenos Aires: Fabril, 1960.

El alhajadito. Buenos Aires: Goyanarte, 1961.

Mulata de tal. Buenos Aires: Losada, 1963. *Mulata* (in English). Tr. by Gregory Rabassa. Boston: Delacorte, 1967.

Páginas de Rubén Darío. Ed. by Miguel Angel Asturias. Buenos Aires: Editorial Universitaria de Buenos Aires, 1963.

Rumania, su nueva imagen. Mexico: Universidad Veracruzana, 1964.

Teatro: Chantaje, Dique Seco, Soluna, La audiencia de los confines. Buenos Aires: Losada, 1964.

"Originalitá e caratteristiche del romanzo latino-americano," *Terzo programma: quaderni trimestrali* No. 4. Turin: Eri Edizioni della Rai Radiotelevisione Italiana, 1964.
Clarivigilia primaveral. Buenos Aires: Losada, 1965.
El espejo de Lida Sal. Mexico: Siglo XXI Editores, 1967.
Latino América y otros ensayos. Introduction by Josué de Castro. Madrid: Guadiana de Publicaciones, 1968.
Maladrón. Buenos Aires: Losada, 1969.

Special Editions

Obras escogidas. 3 vols. Madrid: Aguilar (Colección Joya), 1955, 1961, 1966.
Obras completas. 3 vols. Madrid: Aguilar (Colección Premio Nobel), 1968.

SECONDARY SOURCES

ABREU GÓMEZ, ERMILO. "Poet of Guatemala," *Américas* (Washington, D. C., July 1950). pp. 37–38. On his poetry in English.
ANDERSON IMBERT, ENRIQUE. "Análisis de *El Señor Presidente*," *Testigo* No. 4 (Buenos Aires, December 1966). pp. 1–7. This perceptive and exacting Latin American critic judges the novel to be among the best of Latin America.
Anonymous. Interview. *Repertorio americano* XLVI (San José, March 1, 1950), pp. 82–83. On Maya Quiché literature and culture, and on Latin American writers.
BELLINI, GIUSEPPE. *La narrativa di Miguel Angel Asturias.* Milan: Istituto Editoriale Cisalpino, 1966. Interesting analysis of his fiction, chiefly from the sociopolitical viewpoint.
———. Ed. and Tr. *Parla il Gran Lengua di Miguel Angel Asturias.* Parma: Guanda, 1965. A selection of poems in the original Spanish and in Italian, translated with introduction and notes by Bellini.
CAMPOS, JORGE. Interview. *Insula* XII No. 133 (Madrid, December 1957), p. 4. Asturias says his favorite works are *El Señor Presidente* and *Hombres de maíz.* On the difference between Spanish and Latin American literature.
CASTELPOGGI, ATILO JORGE. *Miguel Angel Asturias.* Buenos Aires: Mandrágora, 1961. An enthusiastic commentary on all his works including poetry.
CORRALES EGEA, JOSÉ. Interview. *Insula* VIII No. 93 (Madrid, September 1953), pp. 2, 4. On the development of Latin American literature and the qualities its writers should have.

――――. Interview. *Insula* XVIII No. 197 (Madrid, April 1963), p. 12. On the social role of Latin American novelists.

DONAHUE, FRANCIS. "Miguel Angel Asturias: su trayectoria literaria," *Cuadernos hispanoamericanos* (Madrid, June 1965), pp. 507–527. An informative article on his life and critics.

FRANKLIN, RICHARD L. "Observations on *El Señor Presidente* by Miguel Angel Asturias," *Hispania* XLIV (December 1961), pp. 683–85. On the novel's metaphysical content.

HARSS, LUIS and DOHMANN, BARBARA. *Into the Mainstream: Conversations with Latin-American Writers*. New York: Harpers, 1967, pp. 68–101. Based on interviews, this chapter is informative on Asturias' thought, but commentary on the novels and plays reveals an extremely cursory reading of them.

LORENZ, GÜNTER W. "Hearing the Scream." Interview. Tr. *Die Welt*, in *Atlas: A Window on the World* XIV No. 6 (New York, December 1967), pp. 56–58. On his social novels, magic realism, the Spanish American writer, books to come, and the difficulties of translating his works.

LYON, THOMAS E. "Miguel Angel Asturias: Timeless Fantasy," *Books Abroad* Spring (Norman, Oklahoma, 1968), pp. 183–89. A fresh insight into the telluric and mythic qualities of Asturias' work (pp. 186–87), and the admirable correspondence of his style.

MEAD, ROBERT G., JR. *Saturday Review* (New York, November 4, 1967), p. 32. Review of the English translation of *Mulata de tal*.

MENTON, SEYMOUR. *Historia crítica de la novela guatemalteca*. Guatemala: Editorial Universitaria, 1960, pp. 195–241. The chapter on Asturias is an informative pioneer study, used as a springboard for much subsequent criticism.

MORRIS, IRA. Interview. *La revue de Paris* (February 1968), pp. 99–104. Speaks of magic, surrealism, coming books.

NAVARRO, CARLOS. "La hipotiposis del miedo en *El Señor Presidente*," *Revista iberoamericana* XXXII(Pittsburgh, 1966), pp. 51–61. Fear, expressed and magnified through sensorial perceptions (absolute obscurity, strident noises, etc.), is seen to be the true essence and chief protagonist of the novel.

NAVAS RUIZ, RICARDO. "Tiempo y palabra en Miguel Angel Asturias," *Quaderni iberoamericani* IV No. 29 (Turin, December 1963), pp. 276–82. On time in *El Señor Presidente* and the stylistic portrayal of it. Also contained in the following publication:

――――. *Literatura y compromiso: ensayos sobre la novela política hispanoamericana*. São Paulo: Universidade de São Paulo, 1963. In comparing various political novels, this booklet finds that Valle-Inclán's *Tirano Banderas* (often said to be Asturias' model) is formally

artistic, but false in content, whereas a masterful balance of matter
and form is achieved in *El Señor Presidente*. A fine study, but not
widely available.

PÉREZ, GALO RENÉ. "Miguel Angel Asturias," *Americas* (Washington,
D. C. January 1968), pp. 1–5. Article in English; finds that the first
four chapters of *El Señor Presidente*, concerning the city beggars and
the idiot Pelele's agony, contain the principal elements developed in
subsequent chapters. Pérez does not say so, but his work suggests
that this world of derelicts, warped, terrorized, and cruelly selfish,
reflects in microcosmic caricature the moral disease of the whole
subjugated society.

PILON, MARTA. *Miguel Angel Asturias: semblanza para el estudio de su
vida y obra con una selección de poemas y prosas.* Guatemala: Cultural
Centroamericana, 1968. Written to acquaint Guatemalan students
with their famous native son, this book contains details about his
life, pictures of him since childhood, and other items of personal
interest.

SÁNCHEZ, LUIS ALBERTO. *La tierra del quetzal.* Santiago de Chile: Ercilla,
1950. Excellent introduction to Maya and Guatemalan background.
Although few pages are devoted to Asturias, Sánchez was the first
critic to discern his genius, predicting that in time he would become
a major classic.

WEST, ANTHONY. *The New Yorker* (March 28, 1964), pp. 158–60. Sin-
gularly perceptive review of the English translation of *El Señor
Presidente*.

An abundance of studies is springing up in the once semiarid landscape
of Asturian criticism as a result of the Swedish academy's salutary perspi-
cacity. A thorough and invaluable critical bibliography of works by and
about Asturias was collected and published by Pedro F. de Andrea in
Revista iberoamericana, No. 67 (Pittsburgh, Jan.-Apr. 1969), pp. 135–267.

Index

Adonis, 40; Venus and, 34, 51, 64–65
Alberti, Rafael, 163
Alegría, Ciro, 13
anima, 76, 78–83, 90–92, 117,
129–30, 138–39, 161–62, 171; definition, 90; negative, 91, 92,
161–62, 171
Annals of the Cakchiquels, 12, 72,
123
Arbenz, President Jacobo, 154
Arévalo, President Juan José, 12
Asturias, Blanca Mora Araujo de
(his wife), 13
Asturias, Miguel Angel, life, 11–13;
in Bolivia, 155; interest in occultism, 53; power of characterization, 89, 117, 164; views on
Latin American literature,
13–17; drama, 120–51; essays,
163–64; short stories, 152–60,
173; *El alhajadito*, 161; *La audiencia de los confines*, 131–35,
150–51; banana trilogy, 14,
85–119; *Carta aérea a mis amigos
de América*, 173; *Chantaje*,
135–39, 147–50; *Cuculcán*,
123–24, 147; *Dique seco*, 139–50;
El espejo de Lida Sal, 152–54;
"Leyenda de las Tablillas que
Cantan," 153–54; *Hombres de
maíz*, 53–84, 90, 117, 125, 127,
130, 146, 153, 164; *Leyendas de
Guatemala*, 123, 152–53; *Maladrón*, 162–63; *Mulata de tal*,

161–62, 164; *Los ojos de los enterrados*, 12, 85, 112–19, 156; *El
papa verde*, 14, 85, 97, 164; *El
Señor Presidente*, 16, 18–52, 66,
74, 97, 157, 159, 163; *Soluna*,
124–31, 142, 146, 147–50; *Viento
fuerte*, 85–96, 103, 130; *Week-end
en Guatemala*, 112, 154–60, "El
Bueyón," 155, "Torotumbo,"
154, 156–60
Attis, 81; and Cybele, 34, 62–64,
65, 81, 173
Aztec, myths and legends, 171;
Huitzilopochtli (sun), 66; Nanahuatl (sun), 117, 172; Tlazolteotl, 66, 68; Toci, 68, 120;
Xochiquetzal, 67; *see also* Quetzalcoatl

Babylon, 34, 52, 169; myths and
legends, 33–52; Tyche (Fortuna),
44–45; *see also* Ishtar
Bacchus, *see* Dionysus
Barba Jacob, Porfirio, 163
Bellini, Giuseppe, 6, 159, 169
Bergman, Ingmar, *Persona*, 173
Bible, 122; *Apocalypse*, 52; *Daniel*,
37; *Ezekiel*, 40, 44; Jonas, 143;
Song of Songs, 25–26, 37
Bourguignon, Serge, *Les dimanches
et Cybèle*, 173

Carpentier, Alejo, *Tientos y diferencias*, 168

Castelpoggi, Atilio, 159
Castillo Armas, Colonel Carlos, 154, 155
Chilam Balam, books of, 13, 123
Christ, the age of, 128, 146; and bad thief, 162
Cisneros, Ximénez de, 132
consciousness, development of, 5, 46, 71, 75–76, 128–31, 137–39, 147–48; early stage, 78–80, 137–38; heroic stage, 46, 78–79, 138–39; *see also* individuation
corn gods and myths, *see* fertility myths
Cybele, 47; *see also* Attis and Cybele

Darío, Rubén, 163
descent to the underworld, 44, 63, 77–82, 117
Dickens, Charles, 164
Dionysus (Bacchus), 40, 60–61, 62f., 65

Earth Mother, 41–43, 50, 73–75, 78, 81, 109, 120, 128
Egyptian, myths and legends, 120, 143–47; Horus, 143, 145; Set, 143–44; *see also* Osiris
Eliade, Mircea, 70
Estrada Cabrera, President Manuel, 11, 119, 167

feminine principle, 79–80, 83, 129–31; attributes, 76, 91
fertility, theme in *El Señor Presidente*, 23–32; in *Hombres de maíz*, 71ff.; in "Torotumbo," 159–60
fertility myths, Asia Minor, 62–64, 65, 78; Aztec, 66–68, 172; Babylon, 33–52; Egyptian, 69–70, 143–47; Greek, 60–62, 64–65, 68–69, 76; Maya, 63, 107–11,

120–22, 168; Mediterranean, 60–66; meaning, 34, 46, 75, 120, 150
Freud, Sigmund, 33

Gallegos, Rómulo, 13
García Lorca, Federico, 163
German, myths and legends, Faust, 82, 161; Wotan, 50
Girard, Rafael, 122–23, 168, 170, 172
Goethe, J. W., 82
Great Mother (Magna Mater), 37f, 41–47, 51–52, 61–63, 66–68, 75–76, 78–83, 137–39, 143; symbols of, 37f., 46, 169
Greece, myths and legends, Circe, 47, 91, 92; *Dionysia*, 60–62; Hermes, 65; Persephone, Demeter, and Pluto, 61–62, 68–69; Minotaur and Theseus, 46, 76, 81; *taurobolium*, 64; Tyche (Fortuna), 44–45; *see also* Adonis, Dionysus

Harss, Luis, 53
hero myth, 138–39; Theseus, 46, 76, 81
Herodotus, 35
Hunahpú (corn god), 62–63, 83, 109–11, 168
Hun-Hunahpú (agrarian god), 117; and Xquic, 109–11, 168
Huracán, 94–95, 108–11

Indian (American), world view, 15, 74, 123, 162, 164–65; *see also* Maya, Aztec
individuation (maturation), 77–78, 79, 80, 128–31; *see also* Self
initiation, *see* rebirth
Ionesco, Eugene, *Victimes du devoir*, 173

Ishtar, 168, 169; and Tammuz, 34–51
Isis, *see* Osiris and Isis

Joyce, James, 33
Jung, Carl Gustav, 33; depth psychology, 5, 46–52, 70, 71, 75–84, 90–93, 121, 128–31, 137–39, 146–51, 153, 172, 173; *Symbols of Transformation*, 51, 171, 172

Kepner, C. D., Jr., and Soothill, J. H., *The Banana Empire: a Case Study in Economic Imperialism*, 95–96, 107

Las Casas, Bishop Bartolomé de, 131–35
Lenin Peace Prize, 12
literature, Latin American, 13–17, 33–34, 165–66; Maya, 6, 12, 13, 16, 33, 48, 107, 110, 120–23, 168, 170; of protest, 13–14, 119, 166
Lorenz, Günter W., 6, 13

magic realism, 17, 162
Mary, Virgin, 43, 47
masculine principle, 129, 131; attributes, 76
Maya, myths and legends, 16, 54, 57–58, 71–73, 92, 107–11, 120–24, 168, 170; Gucumatz (Cuculcán), 107, 108, 123–24; Tohil, 28, 49–50; Votan, 109; Xmucané, 83, 108, 111, 168; Xtabay, 111, 117; sacred ball game, 110
Méndez Montenegro President Julio César, 12
myths, truth of, 56, 70, 74, 116, 160; *see also* fertility myths

nahual, 37, 58, 63, 127, 130, 131
Neruda, Pablo, 12

night sea journey, 77, 146; *see also* descent to the underworld
Nobel Prize (Asturias), 12, 150, 162
non-violence, 114–15, 158

Osiris, 62; as Nile, 69, 143; and Isis, 34, 69–70, 143–48

palo volador, 120, 122
Popol Vuh, 12, 107, 110, 122, 123, 168, 170
psychic energy (libido), 50, 81, 92; and sacrifice, 75, 127–28

Quetzalcoatl, 66–68
Quixote, Don, 133; and Dulcinea, 171

Rabinal Achí, 120–22, 137
Raynaud, Georges, 6, 12, 72, 121, 164, 172
rebirth (renewal), 30, 31, 34, 36, 63–64, 75–84, 128–31, 141, 144, 146, 169; symbols of, 39, 128; *see also* fertility myths
Reyes, Alfonso, 6
Rivera, José Eustasio, *La vorágine*, 15

sacrifice, 28, 32, 49–50, 73–77, 80–83, 108, 121–22, 127–28, 146, 171; definition, 75, 81, 127
Sánchez, Luis Alberto, 21, 53, 170
satan (devil, Beelzebub), 39, 40, 65–66, 161
Self, 78, 128, 130, 131, 148, 169; realization, 147–48; symbols of, 131; see also individuation
serpent, symbol of fertility, 45–46, 61, 109; tail-eating, 46–48; Guatemalan, 39, 157; feathered, 66, 107
shadow, 129–30

Shakespeare, William, 25–26, 45
Solórzano, Carlos, 124
Stein, Gertrude, 163
Steinbeck, John (*The Grapes of Wrath*), 119
sun gods and myths, *see* fertility myths and legends
Surrealism, 26, 28, 148

Tam Lin (English legend), 101, 109
Tammuz, see Ishtar
Terrible Mother, 41ff., 47–48, 76–77, 79, 138–39, 146; as Tohil, 50–51; as Babylon, 52
time, 21, 63, 124, 153, 154, 158
transformation, *see* rebirth
Twain, Mark, 152

Ubico, Jorge, 12
unconscious, 50, 63, 91–93, 138,

150, 160, 169, 172; dreams and visions, expression of, 54, 71, 74, 95, 127–29, 149; myths, expression of, 46, 50, 71; personification of, 46f, 80–81; symbols of, 58, 76, 91, 129, 169; lure of, 63, 76, 81, 91
United Fruit Co., 85, 95–96, 100, 107
Uroborus, 46–48, 137, 148

Valéry, Paul, 153
Venus (Aphrodite), *see* Adonis

wise old man, 78, 170, 171; definition of, 75, 92–93, 130

Xquic, *see* Hun-Hunahpú